Badminton B For Complete Beginners

Montyf O Chana

The benefits of taking up badminton

In addition to extending life and improving mobility, badminton also encourages cardiac health and physical activity for people of all ages and abilities.

Learn more about the advantages of including badminton in your monthly fitness routine here:

A total-body workout is badminton.

Playing a game of badminton can help you expend about 450 calories per hour as you lunge, dive, run, and get your heart pumping. The various motions work your entire body, including your hamstrings, quads, calves, and core, to give you a strong cardio exercise.

Socialising

We advise people to exercise five times a week for 30 minutes. Some of us may be culpable of not exercising as often as we ought to because of growing obligations at home and at work. The sport of badminton is enjoyable and adaptable, allowing you to fit it into your busy timetable. Our courts are open for rental throughout the day, night, and on weekends. You can even socialize and meet up with friends and family during your workout.

Tennis Enhances Your Mental Health

Engaging in any regular physical exercise encourages the release of endorphins, which are our body's natural feel-good, happy hormones. In turn, this can enhance our general mood and sleep while lowering tension, anxiety, and depression. Badminton is a social sport because it encourages player interaction and teamwork in solo and doubles rallies. For senior players, this can be especially helpful in overcoming loneliness.

Heart Wellness

Your body must have a healthy heart in order for it to operate effectively. Badminton raises the amounts of good cholesterol and lowers the levels of "bad" cholesterol, which can narrow your blood vessels. As a result, there is a lower chance of heart attack, stroke, and hypertension (high blood pressure).

Badminton Aids in Lowering Health Risks

Playing badminton can lower your chances of getting type two diabetes as an adult. It lessens the liver's ability to produce sugar, which lowers the body's basal blood sugar.

While chasing the shuttlecock and moving quickly around the court can help children and young adults build bone mass and density. Osteoporosis is less likely to develop in the future as a result.

Longer Life Expectancy

According to a 9,000-person study from Denmark, practicing a racket sport like badminton can add about six years to your life expectancy. While riding, swimming, and jogging can all add over three years to life expectancy, football can extend it by more than four.

Enhanced Mobility

Our mobility progressively deteriorates as we get older. By making sure we lubricate our joints and maintain a busy lifestyle, we can stop this from happening. Additionally, it lowers the chance of developing gout and other joint conditions.

Badminton is a Versatile Sport

No matter your physical condition or fitness level, anyone can appreciate badminton. By changing the tempo at which you're performing, you can select a more or less demanding workout. This is done to accommodate both your particular needs and the requirements and skills of the other participants.

Family Friendly

Kids are using smart phones, tablets, and TVs as forms of amusement as they become more tech savvy. It can occasionally be challenging to inspire your kids to leave the house and engage in physical exercise after school.

You can teach them the value of exercise and health while also teaching them new skills by taking them to a badminton match. Additionally, your entire family will be able to enjoy yourselves greatly.

Health Without Brain Is Nothing

It's fascinating to consider how playing badminton is good for the mind. The majority of badminton's bodily health advantages are clear-cut and foreseeable. But have you ever had a dream that you felt wonderful while exercising your brain? Yes, that is accurate. Endorphins, a neurotransmitter that makes your brain feel good and happy, are produced during a tight badminton battle. Unusual, but accurate.

You're Intelligent Enough

Badminton is a game of strategy. It requires preparation for where to aim, how to serve, what kind of smash to use, when to return, and other details. It also requires coordination between your intellect and senses. As a result, it compels your sleepy brain to get up and work. You will undoubtedly become a cunning, clever lad as a result.

Your Reflex Action Is Increased

Being a quick activity, it necessitates both quick physical and mental reflexes from one to the other. You have to physically change from one to the other in a matter of seconds, and you also have to think quickly and accurately recall the shots. These quick reflexes improve your everyday thinking and living as well.

Contents

CHAPTER 1

Thoughts about learning

1.1. A little about learning theory

We all learn and develop continuously throughout our whole lives. In other words, we can`t choose NOT to learn and develop.

Fundamentally, this is because learning with a fancy word is an "adaptive process", which means that through learning and development, we become able to adjust and adapt to the different demands and expectations important in the specific context we in a given moment are a part of. You can say that to survive both metaphorically and literally, we have to be able to learn and adapt. For example, my students in the sports science study at the University of Aalborg have to learn the curriculum in the different courses and projects they are part of, to be able to pass the exams. In other words, they have to learn and adapt to survive as students.

Learning as a necessity to survive literally is also relevant and important in many situations in our daily lives. For example, we have to learn to look for cars before we cross the road. If we don`t learn this we risk being hit by a car, which probably is not healthy.

Learning as an adaptive process means that we as human beings fundamentally are motivated for learning, to survive both metaphorically and literally.

Learning in the short thus is the same as "change". Furthermore, it is a detectable change, which means, that when a person has learned something, we can see a change in the behaviour of the person. This definition tells us when learning has taken place, and all scientists agree on this, no matter how they look at and explain different learning approaches. We as badminton coaches, in this perspective, can see if our players have learned something from the training, we are doing with them. If a specific player plays in the exact same way after the training as she did before, it indicates that the player didn`t learn anything from the training.

With the above in mind, it makes no sense to see players as not motivated for learning. If the players can see the relevance of the training, regarding their potential for development, the motivation for learning per definition will be present. In other words, it`s about the player can see the possibility to "survive", or in other words, improve their competencies to succeed in the environment she is part of. If the players can`t see the relevance of the input and specific exercises they are working with, they per definition will not be motivated and interested in the training, and therefore probably not learn anything.

From an overall perspective, we talk about 3 fundamental learning theories These are **constructivism, social learning**, and **behaviourism.**

Especially constructivism and social learning will be the focus of this book, regarding how the different exercises are constructed. Behaviourism will be present, as almost all the exercises are small competitions, which is something behaviourism is dealing with.

Constructivism fundamentally is about, how we as individuals construct our knowledge through an inner cognitive process, or in other words through the process of thinking, using what is called "reflection" as the main tool for learning. This will be further discussed in the following chapter, where constructivism will be the theoretical background for examples of exercises aiming at developing reflective competencies.

Social learning is fundamentally about, that we learn through social participation, meaning we learn in situations where we interact with other people, using communication as the main tool for learning. This process will be further discussed in a chapter to come, where I will present exercises aiming at the players will become able to help each other to learn. Also in this chapter, I will present exercises that establish the individual player as an important member of the community, which will develop important competencies for the individual players.

Behaviourism fundamentally is about that we learn through a stimulus-response process, a process where there is no focus on reflection or mental activities in general. A lot of us probably remember Pavlov`s dogs from our high school education. Pavlov who was a Russian behaviourist made his famous experiment, where he trained the dogs to dribble at the sound of a bell because he connected the sound of the bell to the smell of food. As mentioned behaviourism has no focus on reflection or communication, but focuses only on visible behaviour. In other words, behaviourists believe that you can teach and coach using instruction, just telling players what to do, without any interest in what they are thinking and how they perceive the input they are receiving. When this is said, behaviourism plays an important role in our daily lives. For example, we move our hands very fast from a hot hob, without having to think about it. Fundamentally, behaviourism has no big place in this book because I don't think this way of thinking can develop the competencies needed for players to be able to cope for themselves on the court, and at the same time develop and experience the fun the game can give you. There is only one component of the behavioristic theory, which is present in this book. This is the idea of competing and taking part in competitions against other players or teams. In behavioristic theory, the notion of rewards is important, the idea being, that when an individual is rewarded for acting in a good way, the reward will encourage the individual to act in the same next time the situation occurs.

In this book, I use competition as a motivational factor, which I will discuss further in the next chapter.

1.2 Thoughts about sport and competition

Historically sport and competing are closely connected. We compete in football playing matches against other teams, aiming at scoring more goals than the opponent and thereby winning the match. We compete in swimming trying to set the fastest times, as well as we compete in running, jumping, and throwing.

Many people think that the fundamental idea of competing against other people is inappropriate, and something we should try to avoid, because when we compete there will always be winners and losers, and in most cases, there will be more losers than winners.

In this book, however, most of my examples of tactical and mental training exercises will contain an element of competition.

I see the completion in itself as a fantastic tool to motivate the players for taking part and engaging the activities in the training sessions and thereby help facilitate and ensure that the learning process I focus on in the book is taking place. This of course for the players to be able to develop competencies regarding the game itself, as well as experience joy and feel happy when playing badminton.

If you, as a coach is aware, that the competition and the notion of winners and losers never can be the main goal of the exercises and the training, the competition as indicated can be a tool for learning and development. At the same time competitions can be a tool for evaluating if the players are developing according to what the goals of the practice are. Competition in this way is only regarded as a tool for achieving far more important goals, being development, and the feeling of joy and self-esteem connected to this.

For me, the important thing when you use competitions in the daily training is how you talk about the importance of winning and losing. For example, I always use "symbolic" rewards for the winners, so the players know that it`s not that important who wins or loses. A symbolic reward could be, that a winning team doesn`t have to take down the nets after training, which means that they save 15 seconds compared to the losing team. At the same time, we never talk about winners and losers when we evaluate how the teams have dealt with the specific exercises and competitions.

Even if the rewards are "symbolic", the motivational effect of the competition is still very high.

Following this, research shows, that competition is a big motivational factor for a lot of people, but a strong focus on mastery compared to performance in competitions is important to develop intrinsic motivation for the activity itself. In connection with this, research from the University of Copenhagen shows that talented players in different sports become more success full as elite athletes, if they love to compete, but do not focus too much on winning or losing.

It is my own experience, that even though a lot of my exercises in my badminton training contain the element of competition, a strong focus on development can ensure that the players become intrinsic motivated and that the competition element ensures high engagement regarding taking part and involve yourself in the activities in training.

Finally, I normally say, that focusing on winning is not that important. If our priority is the development and becoming better at playing badminton, everything else being equal, you will also win more badminton matches.

In chapter 2, I will offer examples and suggestions for exercises based on a constructivist approach to the training, starting with presenting a little theory about the notion of "reflection"

CHAPTER 2.

Exercises based on a constructivist learning approach

2.1. A little about "reflection"

2.1.1. The notion of reflection – a little theory

As mentioned earlier, learning from a constructivist perspective is taking place through the process of reflection. Most of us of course know this concept, and many of us probably connect it to the concept of "thinking".

The concept of reflection however is about more than just "thinking". The fact is that not all kinds of cognitive activity can be defined and understood as reflection.

John Dewey, who many probably connect to the phrase "learning by doing", and who is one of the most important philosophers inside the notion of reflection says, that as long as we just think of "everything and nothing", without having a specific idea regarding the outcome of the thinking process, then we can`t call the process for reflection.

Reflection only takes place, when we act, and the action doesn`t have the outcome we expected. If you, for example, walk on the sideway and suddenly glide and injure yourself, which is not what usually happens when you walk on a sideway, then you have to figure out what has happened and what you are going to do next time you will have a walk. Probably you know from experience that when there is snow or ice on the sideway, the sideway becomes slippery, and you have to be careful. So the result of this reflection process could be, that next time you walk, you check out if there is snow or ice on the sideway. In other words, the process of reflection means that you consider why you failed, and then use your experiences to figure out how to act in a similar situation in the future, in order not to fail again.

In this perspective, mistakes should be regarded as the tool for learning how to act in a better way in the future. If your actions have the outcome you expect, there is no need for the process of reflection, as our existing knowledge is sufficient to handle a specific situation in a good way. The "mistake", especially in training situations, has to be regarded as a positive event, as this is our only way of learning new things and becoming stronger in the future.

Fortunately, the ability to reflect can be practised. When we find ourselves in situations where we are "forced" to make mistakes, for example, in badminton training, the players will become better and better at accepting making mistakes, and at the same time, through the process of reflection, become better at analyzing what went wrong, and what they should do in similar situations in the future, not to make the same mistakes again.

The ability to reflect, in this way, is important on all levels in badminton, to be able to make good choices on the court. Our opponents will continuously try to change the way they are playing, to prevent our tactic to work. This means, that the players very often will be in situations where things change, and we make mistakes. When this happens, the players have to reflect, as discussed above, to prevent doing the same mistakes in the future.

You could argue that the ability to reflect becomes more and more important the higher level you play. This is because the difference between low-level players and high-level players is exactly the ability to be aware of what the opponent does, and then try to disturb what is working for them.

2.1.2. What then specifically characterizes exercises aiming at developing reflective competencies in badminton?

If you want to train the development of reflective competencies for the players, there are several specific parameters characterizing the exercises.

Overall, you should "force" the players to make mistakes by:

- Change premises and rules in the exercises continuously.

- In general, try to expose the players to new input.

- Develop exercises with in-built changes in premises and rules, for example depending on who wins or loses rallies and games.

- Reward successful reflection processes – for example, do the exercises as small competitions. The reward primarily will be that you win. In these exercises, it is important that winning or losing is not that important compared to developing reflective skills.

- In other words, you should change the content of exercises when the players become too familiar with the demands of the specific exercise.

If you have not worked in this way with your players before, you will probably experience, that the players, in the beginning, become a little frustrated, because they will make mistakes more often than they are used to, which they probably will see as a negative thing. In my own experience, it will however only take a short time before the players will become used to this approach to training, and actually will look forward to exercises like this. The players will, in this way change the criteria of success from being able to avoid making mistakes to finding out how fast they can react to mistakes, and avoid doing the same mistakes more than one time.

A little later in this chapter, I will describe several exercises aiming at developing these reflective competencies.

2.1.3. Communication that facilitates the development of reflective competencies.

The role of the coach, working with the development of reflective skills, is apart from constructing exercises like those described above, also to facilitate that the reflection processes of the players are happening in the right way.

The communication between coach and players is in this perspective deciding if the specific exercises will make the players reflect. As a starting point, the coach should avoid pure instruction telling the players what is wrong and what to do next. Communication, based on instructions is fundamentally behavioristic based, and this approach will not facilitate and develop reflective skills. On the contrary, the players learn to do what they are told, which is not appropriate, as the players when on the court have to make decisions for themselves. Communication facilitating reflective skills should be based on the coach asking questions, aiming at the players themselves to find out why they failed and what to do in the future in similar situations. Specific questions relevant after mistakes have been made could be, "what did you think would happen when you chose this solution"? and "what do you think you can do next time you are in the situation"? The questions should be "open" meaning that they should not be answered with "yes" or "no", as questions like this will not motivate the player to reflect. In other words, the coach shall facilitate the development of reflective skills through a dialogue based on open questions. The coach in the dialogue should make the players curious, using questions for example "your suggestion to a solution is nice, but if I say I would have chosen a different solution, what do you think then"? According to Dewey – yes the guy with the "learning by doing" thing, is curiosity an important parameter regarding the ability to develop reflective competencies.

2.1.4 Development of reflective competencies entails automatically intrinsic motivation.

The most important factor regarding going on playing badminton throughout your whole life, and probably also a condition for becoming a good player, is that the players are motivated for playing badminton. Motivation, however, can take place in several ways. The strongest form of motivation, regarding the possibility to stay in the sport for a lifetime is called intrinsic motivation. When you are intrinsically motivated, you play badminton because you find it fun, and you in this way get experiences you can`t have in other ways. In other words, you don`t play badminton to win tournaments, become a world champion, or to be praised.

According to American psychologists Edward Deci and Richard Ryan, who have developed what they call the "self-determination theory", intrinsic motivation will develop, when the players experience a feeling of "competence, autonomy, and relatedness". In other words, the development of intrinsic motivation demands, that the players fundamentally feel that they have competencies, and feel that they master the different skills needed according to the level of badminton they are playing on. Also, the players have to experience a feeling of autonomy, meaning that the players experience that they are able and allowed to make independent choices on and off the court.

Working from a constructivist-based learning approach, aiming at developing reflective skills as described in this chapter, will develop exactly the feeling of competence and autonomy. Through the reflection process, the players will make their own choices, which will cause the feeling of autonomy – "I can handle things on my own". The reflection process also means that the players on their own are developing new and more appropriate ways of action for the future, which will foster the feeling of competence.

Badminton training based on constructivism and the development of reflective skills, in this way, will develop two of the three parameters necessary to be intrinsically motivated.

The third parameter "relatedness" I will discuss in a later chapter when I describe and discuss exercises from "a social learning perspective".

2.2 Specific exercises developing basic reflective competencies

2.2.1 1 against 1 exercises

Exercise 1:

The court is split up into six areas on each side of the net, as shown in the figure below.

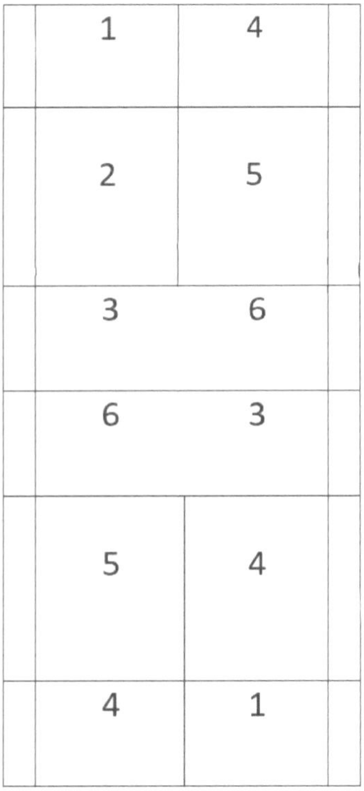

1	4
2	5
3	6
6	3
5	4
4	1

Figure 1

We play singles on a singles court in sets to 3 points. From the start of the exercise, we play on the full single court, including all 6 areas. The loser of the set can subsequently close one of the six areas on his half. Afterwards, we play a new set to 3 points.

The exercise is finished when one of the players has lost six sets, and in this way closed all areas on his own courtside.

The players shall in this exercise reflect upon, what areas would be best to close after a lost set taking into consideration what has happened in the set before. The winner of the previous set will now have to adjust to the situation, and prepare to make new choices, as the court of the opponent now is different from before.

Probably the change of the loser's court will lead to mistakes from the opponent, as the court he now faces is different. This means that the player will have to reflect in the rallies on how to avoid playing to a closed area.

Exercise 2:

The court is split up into six areas on each side of the net, as shown in the figure below.

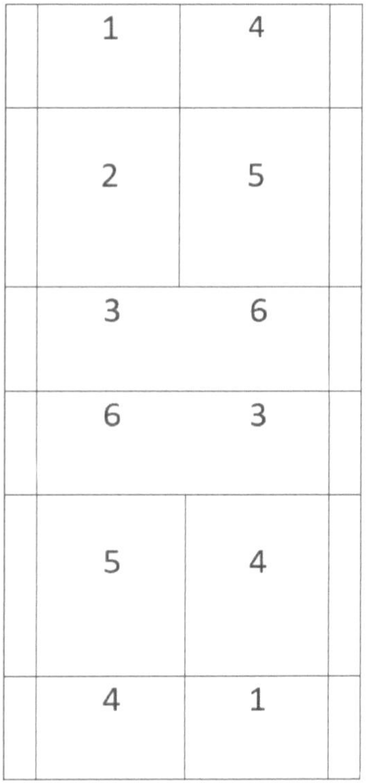

Figure 2.

In this exercise, we again play sets to 3 points. The match is starting with a set of 3 points, and the court in this first set is on consists of area number 2 on both sides of the net. The loser of a set can subsequently open another area on the opponents' side. The exercise is finished when one of the players has lost six sets.

The players have to reflect upon, which areas are the best to open up after a lost set, based on experiences from the sets played before. Both players have to reflect upon and adjust tactics and choices as the court now has changed. The change of conditions probably will lead to more mistakes, which means that the players have to reflect in each rally, on how to avoid new and similar mistakes.

Exercise 3:

We play singles on a singles court, where the player who serves has a court marked by number 2, and the receiver has a court marked by number 1 on the figure below

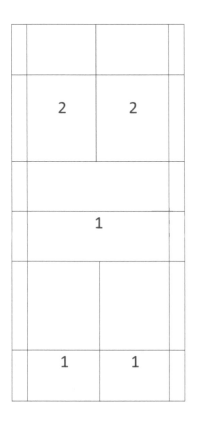

Figure 3

The player serving will now have to play to the opponent`s front and back ditch. The receiver has to play to the opponent`s quarter court between the ditches. When the right to serve shifts, the court of both players will also change. Already before the exercise starts, the players will have to reflect upon how the changed conditions will affect the game, compared to playing on a normal court, and plan how to manage this new situation.

The fact that conditions will change every time the service changes probably will mean that the players make more mistakes than they usually will. Again this means, that they have to reflect upon, how mistakes can be avoided in the rallies to come.

You can play this exercise on time, for example, for 15 minutes, or in short sets to 5 points.

Fundamentally, when doing these kinds of reflection exercises, you should allow the players time to reflect both before rallies and finished sets, and after rallies and sets are finished.

Exercise 4:

In this exercise, we play singles on a singles court. The rule is that every second stroke shall be played to area number 1 and every second stroke shall be played to area number 2, as shown in figure 4 below.

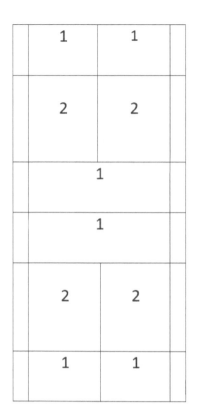

Figure 4.

Probably the players will make mistakes and play in the wrong areas more often than normal, because of the changing conditions. This means, that the players between the rallies have to reflect upon how to play the next rallies to avoid making the same mistakes again.

The exercise can be done on time. I normally do it for 10 minutes. Alternatively, you can play shorts sets to for example 5 points. The reason for the short intervals is that the process of reflection can be exhausting if you do the exercises for too long time. Again, there must be enough time between the rallies to reflect and make new plans, if something has gone wrong in the rally before.

Exercise 5:

In this exercise, we play singles, but on a doubles court. The strokes should be played alternately to areas number 1, 2, and 3, as shown in figure 5.

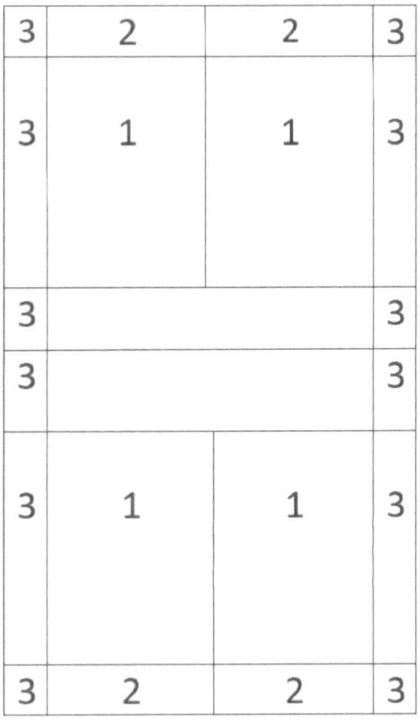

3	2	2	3
3	1	1	3
3			3
3			3
3	1	1	3
3	2	2	3

Figure 5.

As indicated, the players have to play alternately in the middle part of the court, the front, and back ditches, and the side ditches normally part of the double court.

Compared to exercise number 4, the players will probably make more mistakes caused of the higher complexity of the exercise. This means that the demand for reflection is higher, compared to exercise number 4.

Again, the exercise should be done in small sets of 3 or 5 points, or in short time intervals.

Exercise 6:

In this exercise, we play singles, on a singles court with the net only having the same height as the net on a tennis court. This means, that the net will be placed from the floor to the top of the net.

The rallies start with a high service to the backline, to start up the rally in an appropriate way.

The players will probably experience, that they, because of the changed height of the net, will make wrong choices, and therefore have to reflect on how they should handle this new situation.

For example, the players will often have an expectation, that it could be a good idea to attack a lot with full smashes, which they will find out is not always a good idea in this exercise.

Again, you should allow the players to have some extra time between rallies to reflect upon how to play the next rally.

Exercise 7:

In this exercise, we play singles on a singles court, but without any net at all, and with the centerline

being the line between the net posts.

The rallies are starting up with a high service to the backline, for the rally to start up appropriately.

As in exercise 6, the unusual conditions will for sure mean that the players make a lot of bad choices and mistakes. Because of this, the demand for reflection is very high in this exercise. The players have to find a new concept for their game, to succeed in the exercise.

Normally I do this exercise in short sets of 3 or 5 points, or in short intervals. This gives the players time to reflect between sets and rallies.

Exercise 8:

Exercise numbers 6 and 7 can be combined with exercise number 2. This means that you can play with a low net or without a net, while the court is split up into six areas. The exercise starts with the rule that players are only allowed to play the strokes to area 2, as shown in the figure below.

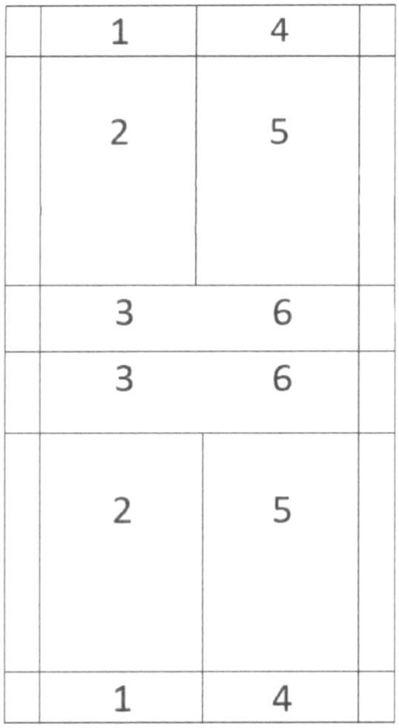

1	4
2	5
3	6
3	6
2	5
1	4

Figure 6.

We play sets to 3 points, and the loser of each set can open up an area on the opponent's half. The rallies start up with a high service to the backline, no matter which areas are open and closed. The match is finished when one of the players has lost six sets.

The demand for reflection in this exercise is extremely high. Because of the very different conditions, the players for sure will make a lot of bad choices and mistakes. This means that they continuously have to reflect upon how they can handle these difficult exercises, to avoid doing the same mistakes too many times.

Exercise 9:

In this exercise, we play singles on a single court, and the net, having a normal height on one side of the court, is sloping towards the other side of the court, ending up being approximately half a meter over the floor. At the low end of the net, it will be in the same position as a tennis net touching the floor.

As the height of the net variates according to where the players are placed on the court, the players will probably experience that they make bad choices and more mistakes than usual, which means that they have to reflect upon how to handle the situation, to avoid making the same mistakes more than one time.

The rallies are starting up with a high service to the backline, and usually, I play small sets to 5 points. The breaks between the sets are being used to talk with the players about how they experienced the situation, and what they plan to do in the next set. In other words, I facilitate the reflection process, as I communicate primarily with questions, as described earlier in this book.

Exercise 10:

Again we play singles on a singles court in this exercise. We play small sets to 5 points. In the first set played, one of the players can only use the net lob stroke one time in a rally. After each set, we switch around, so it now is the other player, who can only use the net lob one time in a rally.

The players of course have to reflect upon when to use the net lob, as this can be used both as an offensive stroke and a defensive stroke.

Usually, I play small sets to 6 to 8 points, using the brakes between the sets to facilitate the reflection process with the players, and at the same time allowing the players time to reflect between rallies.

Exercise 11:

Singles on a singles court. We play small sets to 5 points. In the first set, one of the players can only use a net drop one time in the rally. After each set, we switch around, so it is the other player who can only use the net drop one time in a rally.

Again the players have to reflect upon when to use the net drop, as this probably should be used as an offensive stroke when the player is high on the net.

I use to do exercises 10 and 11 in the same training session, as the fundamental idea in the exercises is the same, but the rules are diametrically opposite, which put up demands on the players' ability to reflect and readiness for change.

As in exercise 10, I usually play sets of 6 or 8 points in this exercise.

Exercise 12:

Singles on a singles court. We play normal singles but without the back ditch being part of the court as shown in figure 7.

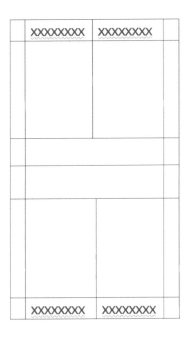

Figure 7.

There will be big demands for reflection in this exercise, as a normal single with a lot of clear and lob shots probably is not a good idea.

As in many of the other exercises until now, I usually play small sets to 3 or 5 points, so that the players, between the sets, have time to reflect on them and talk with the coach about how they can handle this situation.

Normally I play 4 - 6 sets with this exercise.

Exercise 13:

Singles on a singles court. We play small sets to 3 or 5 points. The loser of a set can for the next set chose a specific stroke that the opponent can`t use, for example, "a straight smash from the forehand side".

In this exercise, the players have to reflect on a continuous basis upon what the opponent succeeded within the previous set, and which stroke should be eliminated in the next. Also, the players have to develop new tactics between each set, as the conditions will change dramatically. The demands for reflection in this exercise are very high, and the exercise in this way is developing the reflective skills of the players efficiently.

In all these reflection exercises the players must have time and the possibility to reflect both during the rallies, between the rallies, and between the sets. In this light, it`s important that the coach allows a little longer brakes between rallies and sets. Also, it`s important that the coach facilitate the reflection process through dialogue and questions to the players

Exercise 14:

Singles on a singles court. Both players shall in, each rally make a stroke with the "wrong" or "non-dominant" hand. This stroke can´t be a service or a service return. The task of the players is in this way to reflect upon when you can use the stroke with the "wrong" without being punished by the opponent. If a player loses the rally without the opponent having used the "wrong" hand stroke, the rally is a tie.

As in the earlier exercises, I normally play small sets to 3 or 5 points, so there will be a lot of breaks for reflection and discussion with the coach and opponent. I usually also allow time between each rally, so that the players can reflect in these small breaks also.

Exercise 15:

Singles on a singles court in this exercise. As a starting point, the rallies are played using only singles half-court, as the players play on the singles half-court directly opposite of each other. This means, that the players have to use only straight shots. However, each player has one cross-shot available in every rally. The players now have to reflect carefully upon when it is appropriate to use the cross-shot, as this can be used as an offensive shot as well as a defensive shot. Just after one of the players has used their cross-shot, the rally continues on the other half of the court, unless the opponent uses a cross-shot immediately after.

A goal for the players in this exercise could be to force the opponent to use the cross-shot as a defensive shot and thereby improve your own possibility be able to use the cross-shot as an offensive weapon.

Exercise 16:

Single on a singles court again in this exercise. As a starting point, the rallies are played using only the singles half-court, as the players have the half-court diagonally to each other. In other words, the rallies have to be played using only cross shots. Each player, however, has one straight shot available at every rally. The players have to reflect upon when it is most appropriate to use the straight shot, as this can be used in defensive situations as well as in offensive situations. After a player has used his straight shot, the rally continues on the other half, unless the opponent uses a cross-shot directly after.

Again, a goal for the players in this exercise could be to make the opponent use the straight shot in a defensive situation and thereby improve your possibility to use it in an offensive position afterwards.

Exercise 17:

In this exercise, we play 1 against 1. One of the players has a court between the 2 service lines at the backline, while the other player has a court on the front part of the single court, as shown in figure 7 below. The area on the front part of the court can for example be marked with a couple of shuttle tubes.

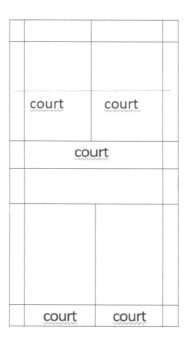

Figure 8.

The game in this exercise will be very much different from normal singles, which will demand a lot of reflection, as the players probably will make wrong choices quite often.

Again, we play short sets to 3 or 5 points, giving the players the possibility to reflect upon what to do next, between the sets.

Usually, I use to let the players change areas between each set, which again makes the demands for reflection even higher.

Exercise 18:

In this exercise, we play a normal net game 1 against 1. As in a traditional net game, the court is from the net to the front service line, as shown in figure 8. Each player however has the opportunity 1 time every rally, to play the shuttle to the area between the 2 service lines at the back, as shown again in figure 9.

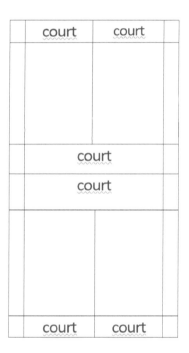

Figure 9.

Again, the game is very different from a normal singles game, which means that the players have to reflect continuously, as they probably will make a lot of bad choices.

The shot to the back ditch can in this exercise be used as an offensive shot, as well as a defensive shot. It could be a goal for the players to use the stroke as an offensive weapon, which can be achieved by forcing the opponent to use the shot in a defensive position.

Again, we play short sets to 3 or 5 points with a 60-minute break between each set, allowing the players time to reflect upon tactics for the following set.

Exercise 19:

In this exercise, we play normal singles. We play short sets to 3 points. Between each set, the players have to try to recall and tell each other how the rallies in the set were played shot by shot. The players also have to recall which choices were good, and which choices were bad.

This exercise specifically trains the ability to do, what we call pro-active reflection, or in other words, the ability to reflect after the situation is finished, to be able to work out new plans and tactics for the next set or the next game.

There is a big difference between players according to how good they are at remembering and reflecting upon what happened in the previous set, but this ability, like everything else, can be trained, using the right kind of exercises.

Exercise 20:

In this exercise, the players are working together two and two. One of the players in the pair plays single against one of the players from the other pair. The player in the pair who is not playing is coaching his partner. The coach can comment on the game between the rallies. There will also be a break between each set so that the coach can talk with his player. We play small sets to 3 or 5 points. After several sets, the roles switch, so each player will be both coaching and playing.

The player who is coaching has to reflect continuously upon what his partner is doing on the court, considering what is working and what is not working. As a consequence of this reflection, the coach has to consider how he would advise his partner to play in the next set.

The role of a coach means, that the players intensively train their reflective competencies.

Exercise 21:

In this exercise, the players are playing singles. Before each set to 3 points, both players write down how they want to approach the set from a tactical perspective, and what they think their opponent will do.

After the set has finished, the coach and the players discuss what happened in the set, and how the players reacted when unexpected things happened.

Finally, both players write down what they think the opponent will do in the next set, and what they plan to do, to be on top of things.

The exercise is a basic exercise practising reflective competencies, as the players have to make plans, evaluate these plans and make new plans for the following set.

Exercise 22:

This exercise is traditionally called "the mirror" in badminton training. In the exercise, we play singles on a normal singles court. One of the players can play like in a normal single. The other player has to be a "mirror", meaning that when his opponent makes a long shot to the backline, the "mirror" has to do a long shot as well. When the opponent does a short shot to the net, the mirror has to do a short shot as well.

The "mirror" can play freely when receiving short serves, and when returning smashes. Also, the "mirror" can kill the shuttle at the net when it`s possible.

In the exercise, the "mirror" primarily has to reflect upon how to avoid losing the rally at the net, while the opponent primarily has to reflect upon how to bring himself into a position where he can make a net kill.

As always in these reflection exercises, we play short sets to 3 or 5 points, allowing extra time also between rallies, so that the players can reflect upon how to handle the situation.

Exercise 23:

This is almost the same exercise as exercise 22. However, the "mirror" in this exercise can deviate one time every rally from being a "mirror". In other words, the "mirror" one time every rally doesn`t have to follow the rules of the "mirror" but can play every shot he wants.

This extra possibility for the "mirror" increase the demand for reflection, as the degree of uncertainty is much higher, compared to exercise 22.

It could be a goal for the "mirror" to use the one deviation offensively, to try to win the rally on this shot. The opponent on the other hand should try to force the "mirror" to do his deviation in a defensive way.

Exercise 24:

In this exercise, we play singles on a singles court. The players can only use underhand shots. This exercise demands a lot, regarding the player`s ability to reflect upon how to handle the situation, as the exercise is different from normal single, regarding both technical and tactical issues.

Again, in this exercise, I normally play short sets to 3 or 5 points, allowing the players to discuss and reflect between the sets, regarding how to handle the next set.

Exercise 25:

Singles on a singles court. In this exercise, the net is lowered, so it has the same height as a tennis net. In other words, the net is fastened to the pole, so it touches the floor.

As in exercise 24, the players can only do underhand shots and the rallies start up with a high single service to the backline.

This exercise is very complex and demands a lot regarding the players' ability to reflect upon how to handle the differences from a normal single.

Like before, I play short sets to 3 or 5 points and also allow extra time between rallies, so that the players have time to reflect, evaluate and adjust their game.

Exercise 26:

The same exercise as 24 and 25, but now the exercise is done without any net at all, and again the players can only use underhand shots.

The rally starts with a long single service to the backline.

This exercise will be extremely challenging for the players, as the demands for reflection are very high, because of the missing net.

As before, we play small sets, with good time between rallies and sets, to reflect upon how to handle the situation.

Exercise 27:

Singles on a singles court. The players have to play this exercise using the "wrong" or the non-dominant hand. In other words, a right-handed player shall use his left hand and the other way around for a left-handed player.

The demands for reflection are very high in this exercise, as the players' technical skills most likely are on a low level, compared to playing with the dominant hand.

Again short sets with plenty of time between rallies and sets for the players to reflect upon this challenge.

In my experience, the players find this exercise very amusing, and sometimes they have had unofficial club champion chips in playing with the "wrong" hand.

Exercise 28:

Singles on a singles court. We play normal singles. The players get 3 points instead of 1, if they can intercept the opponents' clear shots, typically when these are too short or too flat, and afterwards win the rally without giving away the initiative. The players will get 5 points instead of 1 if they win the rally directly on the interception.

When we talk about interception a clear shot it means, that the player intercepting doesn't have to move backwards, before he attacks the opponent's clear shot. Mostly you will attack with a stick smash when intercepting a clear shot, as the speed of the shot is important in this situation because the opponent most likely will be placed at the backline.

The players have to reflect upon if they intercept in the right situations, and what quality their clear shots shall have, in order not to be intercepted by the opponent.

Exercise 29:

Same exercise as 28 but with the addition that the opponent will have 3 points instead of 1 if the player doesn`t win directly on the interception, and at the same time losses the initiative again later in the rally.

Both players have to reflect upon when the right situations for interceptions are, and at the same time try to trick the opponent to try to intercept, playing clear shots which are just a little too high or too long for interceptions to be a good idea.

Usually, I play normal sets in this exercise, as the point-scoring probably will be very fast.

Exercise 30:

Singles on a singles court. The players can only make short or deceptive long serves. The player who in the rally makes the first defensive shot has to stay in defense the rest of the rally.

The exercise put up large demands for reflection, as the premise for the game is different from a normal single.

It`s very important to remember, that when you do exercises like this, which are not tactically smart, compared to the normal game, the players have to be fully aware, that the goal of the practice is developing reflective skills.

Also in this exercise, it would be smart, that the coach and the players define what a defensive stroke is before starting the exercise, to avoid discussions about this during the exercise.

Exercise 31:

Single on a singles court. The rallies start up with a long single-serve to the back line. The players play from the start of the rally defensive shots. The player who makes the first offensive shot shall remain to play offensive shots the rest of the rally. After one of the players has opened up with an offensive shot, the opponent can play as she wants the rest of the rally. If the player makes a mistake or has to give away the initiative after opening up with an offensive shot, the opponent wins the rally. The opponent also wins the rally if he can win the rally when the player is using an offensive shot. This could be in situations when the opponent intercepts a flat clear shot, or kill at the net.

The exercise demands a lot of reflection, regarding when to use the first offensive shot in the rally.

In this exercise, I usually play short sets with plenty of time between rallies and sets, allowing the players time to reflect upon how to handle this situation.

Exercise 32:

Singles on a singles court. The player receiving serve has free play, while the player serving only can make cross shots.

The exercise again demands a lot of reflection from the players regarding how to handle the restrictions described.

We play small sets again to allow time for the players to reflect and adjust tactics between sets.

Exercise 33:

Singles on a singles court. The player receiving serve has free play, while the player serving has to make only straight shots in the rally.

As in exercise 32, the players have to reflect upon how to handle the restrictions described.

Exercise 34:

The same exercise as 32 and 33, but the player serving now has one chance every rally to deviate from the restrictions. In other words, the players serving have one chance every rally to make a straight shot if the restriction is to play all shots cross and one chance to play a cross-shot if the restriction is to play all shots straight.

The demand for reflection in this exercise is very high, compared to exercises 32 and 33, as the complexity in this exercise is much higher than in the exercises before.

Again, we play short sets to allow time between rallies and sets for the players to reflect upon what to do if mistakes have occurred during the game.

Exercise 35

Normally I call this exercise "the king's game". For example, we have 12 players divided into 2 teams that are as equal in strength as possible. Both teams agree before the exercise starts what players are number 1, 2 and down to number 6 in order of strength. After this, the players go to the courts and number 1 on one team play against number 1 on the other team. The exercise can be done on half or full court, depending on the number of players.

The players now play single matches on time, for example, 2 minutes. After each match, the winner moves a half or a full-court towards the court where number 6 started, and the loser moves a half or a full-court towards where number 1 started the exercise. The goal is to finish on the court players with number 6 started, as this indicates that you won a lot of matches. The winner on the court where number 6 started, stays on this court after winning the match, and the loser on the court where number 1 started, stays on this court after losing a match.The fact that the players get new opponents at short intervals means, that the demand for reflection is big.

You could make differentiations in this exercise so that the weaker players get a point advantage when playing against the better players.

Exercise 36:

This is a "kings game" like in the previous exercise. I always try to do this exercise when I can make 2 teams without any big difference in strength between all the players.

Again we play a single on half or full court, depending on the number of players, and the players move half or a full-court in one direction when they win a match, and the same in the other direction when they lose a match. The rules of the different courts are in this exercise different from each other. If we for example have 4 half or full courts, the first court could be normal rules, the second court could be box/quarter court, the third court could be the area in front of the front service line and between the 2 service lines on the backline and the fourth court could be the sideline ditch.

The exercise demands a lot of reflective skills, as the players have to relate to both new opponents and at the same time to new rules of the game.

2.2.2 2 against 1 exercises

Exercise 37:

This exercise I call "the mirror", as I also mentioned earlier in this chapter.

We play on a singles court in this exercise, and the 2 players on one side are playing a half-court each, and are not allowed to hit the shuttle in the partner's half.

The player who is alone can play a normal free game, while the 2 players have to "mirror" what the alone does. If the player plays to the back line they also have to play to the back line If he plays a short shot to the net, they also have to play a short shot back.

The 2 players can play how they want when receiving a short serve and returning heavy smashes from the player who is alone. Also, they can kill at the net, if they have a chance to do it.

The exercise is demanding for all 3 players, as the premise of the game is very different from a normal game, which means that they probably will make tactical mistakes and have to reflect upon how to play the exercise optimally.

Exercise 38:

Again a 2 against 1 mirror exercise as in exercise 37.

The difference in this exercise is, that the 2 players playing together each are allowed to deviate 1 time every rally from playing the mirror. For example, they can choose to play a shot to the backline if the player alone played a shot to the net, or they can attack with an offensive shot one time in the rally.

The demands for reflection are higher, compared to exercise 37, as what happens in the exercise is much more unpredictable because of the increased possibilities in the game.

Exercise 39:

Again, we play 2 against 1 on a singles court. The 2 players playing together have to hit the shuttle on shift, like in table tennis double.

As the rules are very different from the normal game of single and double, the players on both sides of the net will have to reflect upon how to handle the situation.

You could, for example, play this exercise without the players being allowed to do full smashes, especially if the level of the players is not that high.

Exercise 40:

The idea in this exercise is the same as in exercise 39. The difference is, that the players have to make exactly 2 shots after each other, and after this, the partner has to make also 2 shots – and so on.

Again, the exercise will demands reflection as the premises of the game is so much different from the normal game.

Exercise 41:

2 against 1 exercise. Same idea as in exercise 39, which means that the 2 playing together have to play the shots on shift. The court, however, is different now, as we play on the quarter court, as shown in figure 10.

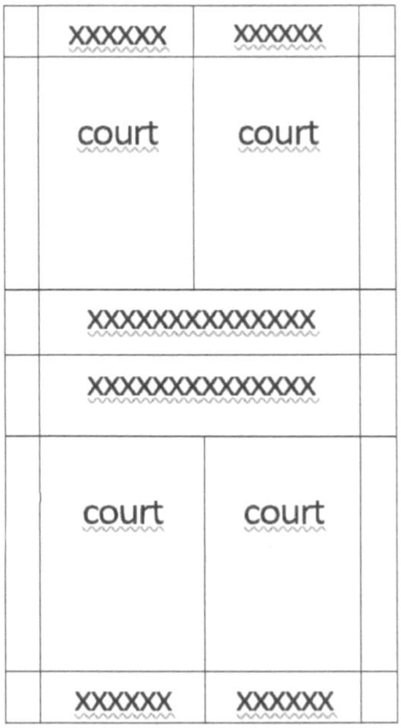

```
┌───┬─────────┬─────────┬───┐
│   │ xxxxxx  │ xxxxxx  │   │
│   ├─────────┼─────────┤   │
│   │         │         │   │
│   │  court  │  court  │   │
│   │         │         │   │
│   ├─────────┴─────────┤   │
│   │  xxxxxxxxxxxxxx    │   │
│   ├───────────────────┤   │
│   │  xxxxxxxxxxxxxx    │   │
│   ├─────────┬─────────┤   │
│   │         │         │   │
│   │  court  │  court  │   │
│   │         │         │   │
│   ├─────────┼─────────┤   │
│   │ xxxxxx  │ xxxxxx  │   │
└───┴─────────┴─────────┴───┘
```

Figure 10.

The tempo in the exercise will compared to exercise 39 be much higher, which will be more demanding regarding the need for reflection.

Again, I suggest, that we play short sets with breaks for discussion and reflection.

Exercise 42:

Again, we play 2 against 1 on a singles court. All 3 players can play freely as they want inside the normal rules. For the 2 players playing together, the restriction is, that each player can hit a maximum of 2 shots after each other, meaning he can choose to hit 1 or 2 shots, after which his partner has to hit the next shot or the next 2 shots.

The exercise is very demanding regarding the need for reflection, as the restrictions probably will mean, that the players will experience a lot of confusion, and will have to reflect upon how to handle this exercise.

Exercise 43:

2 against 1 on a singles court. The 2 players playing together have only 1 racket available, and after 1 of the players has made a shot, he has to give the racket to his partner.

A simple little exercise, in which the demands for reflection are quite high, as the premise of the game is very different from normal badminton.

Exercise 44:

2 against 1 on a singles court. The 2 players playing together much in each rally hit 1 stroke with the "wrong" hand if they should be able to win a point from the rally.

If the 2 players win the rally without having used the 2 shots with the "wrong" hand, the rally will be a tie.

If the player playing alone wins the rally, he will get 1 point no matter what else has happened in the rally.

This exercise demands a lot of reflection from the players. The player who is alone has to reflect upon how he can avoid the opponents can use the shots with the "wrong hand. The 2 players have to reflect upon how and when they can use the strokes with the "wrong" hand, without losing the rally directly after these shots.

As always in these exercises, it is a good idea to play short sets, so the players have time to reflect between the sets. It is also a good idea to allow a little more time between rallies for discussion and reflection.

Exercise 45:

Again 2 against 1 on a singles court. The 2 players playing together only can do 1 net lob shot at each rally. However, they are allowed to kill the shuttle at the net, if they can.

The demands for reflection in this exercise are high, as all 3 players have to relate to and reflect upon how to handle the restriction in the best way possible. The player who is alone has to reflect on how he can make the 2 players use their lob shots from a defensive position, to be able to win the point at the net later in the rally. The 2 players, on the other side, have to reflect upon how they can bring themselves into a position where they can use the lob shots in offensive positions, and maybe win a point directly on the lob shots.

As in the other exercises, we play shorts sets with breaks for discussion and making new plans.

Exercise 46:

This exercise is almost like exercise 45. The difference is that in this exercise the 2 lob shots available for the 2 players playing together can be done by the same player.

The demands for reflection might be a little increased in this exercise compared with exercise 45 because the player playing alone can`t be sure who is going to do the second lob shot, which he could in exercise 45.

Exercise 47:

2 against 1 on a singles court. The 2 players playing together can move around the court as they want. The player playing alone can play how he wants. The restriction of the 2 players is, that they have to play every second stroke to the opponent's quarter court, and every second shot to the opponent's front or back ditch, as shown in figure 11.

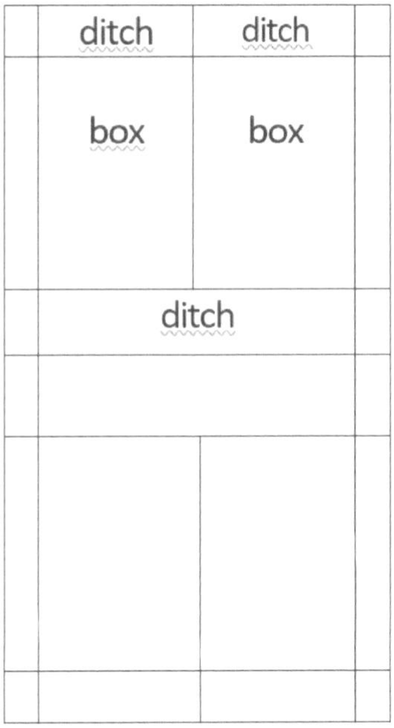

Figure 11.

The exercise demands a lot of reflection, especially regarding the 2 players playing together, as they have to be able to remember in what area they played the previous shot.

Again, we play short sets with breaks between, so the players have time to reflect.

Exercise 48:

2 against 1 on a singles court. The restriction in this exercise is, that the 2 players have to make all shots cross. The players alone can play how he wants.

As the premise of the game is different from normal badminton, a lot of reflection I needed, to handle the restrictions in a good way.

Usually, I play short sets in these exercises, and we must rotate in the exercises, so all players will experience the different roles, and have to reflect upon different problems.

Exercise 49:

This is almost the same exercise as exercise 48. The difference is, that in this exercise each of the 2 players playing together can deviate 1 time every rally from playing cross shots. In other words, each of the 2 players can use 1 straight shot every rally.

Compared to exercise 48 the demands for reflection are much higher, as the degree of uncertainty is much higher.

2.2.3 2 against 2 exercises

Exercise 50:

The most classical 2 against 2 exercise is probably what we in Denmark call "English double".

In the exercise, the players play all against all, and the players have each their half-court, most time to the doubles sideline, as shown in figure 11. The players can`t return the shuttle when it is clearly in another player's half.

Figure 12.

The players can play how they want. However, we play with the "gentleman" rule, meaning that if a player gets a very easy chance of killing the shuttle, he has to kill it at the opponent who made the previous shot. This prevents the players' from rat together against each other.

English double can be played with many different scoring systems. Often the players start with having 5 "eggs", and every time a player losses a rally, he also will lose an egg. When a player has lost all his eggs, he is out of the game, and the remaining players continue. The game is over when there is only 1 player left.

The exercise demands a lot of reflection because of the different premises of the game, and also because the relevance of choices the players can make will shift almost every rally, among other things because the number of players in the exercise will be lower during the game.

Exercise 51:

English double as in exercise 50. In this exercise, the players start with having 3 eggs, and every time a player loses a rally, she will lose an egg. When a player has no eggs left, she is out of the game. The exercise continues till there is only 1 player left.

Compared to exercise 50, the difference is, that every time a player loses an egg, she can remove 1 of the 3 areas on her court, as shown in figure 12. The 3 areas are 1) front ditch, 2) quarter court or 3) back ditch. The opponents are not allowed to play in the selected area for the rest of the game.

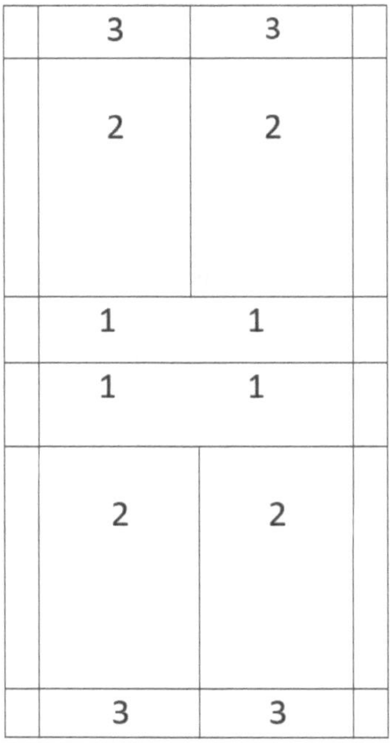

Figure 13.

The exercise demands more reflection than normal English double, because of the changes in court size and premises of the game.

Exercise 52:

Again, we play English double, with all players having their half-court.

In this exercise, however, the net is at tennis height, meaning that the net will be from the floor and up. Like in exercise 50, the players start the game with 5 eggs, and every time a player loses a rally, she will lose an egg. When you have no more eggs left, you are out of the game. The game continues until there is only 1 player left.

The rally starts with a long service, to get the rally started in a good way.

Compared to English double with a normal net height, this exercise will be much harder, regarding the demands for reflection. This is because the premises of the game are so different, which probably will increase the number of mistakes and bad decisions.

Exercise 53:

This exercise is almost the same as exercise 52. The difference is that we are now playing without a net, and the middle line is the line between the net posts.

We have the same rules regarding point scoring as in exercise 52, and again we start the rallies up with a long serve.

Compared to exercises 50 and 52, this exercise will increase the demand for reflection even more, as the premises of the game are so different from normal badminton.

In my experience, the players find exercises with different heights of the net both fun and challenging, because they have to reflect and use their imagination to solve the problems in the exercises.

Exercise 54:

In this exercise, the players play together 2 and 2 like in a normal double. However, the players` have each their half-court as in English double, and they are not allowed to return the shuttle from the partners' half of the court.

In the exercise, the pair serving have to play all shots straight, and the pair receiving serve can play as they want.

Again, there will be demands for reflection, as the premise of the game is very different from normal badminton.

We play short sets to 5 points so the players will have the opportunity to reflect upon how they dealt with the previous set, and come up with a plan for the next set.

Exercise 55:

In this exercise, the players, as in exercise 54, play together 2 and 2 like in a normal double. However, the players` have each their half-court as in English double, and they are not allowed to return the shuttle from the partners' half of the court.

The pair serving have to play all shots cross, and the pair receiving serve can play as they want.

Compared to exercise 54, the demands for reflection probably will be higher in this exercise, as it often is more difficult to make cross shots than straight shots, which means, that the players have to think carefully about how they deal with this exercise.

Exercise 56:

Again, we play 2 against 2, with the same rules as in exercises 54 and 55. The difference in this exercise is, that each player in the pairs has 1 opportunity to deviate from the rule saying that the pair serving has to play either straight or cross.

Compared to exercises 54 and 55, this exercise will demand more regarding the need for reflection, as the players probably will make more bad choices because of the change in premises.

Exercise 57:

This exercise is almost like exercise 56. The pair in the rally still have 2 possibilities to deviate from playing straight or cross. However, it is allowed for 1 of the players to do both shots that deviate, and it`s still a possibility for the players in the pair to do 1 deviation each.

The demands for reflection in this exercise will be higher, compared to exercise 56, because of the change in the premise.

Exercise 58:

2 against 2 on a singles court. The players on the same side of the net are playing together against the other pair. We play with normal point-scoring.

The players in the pair have to hit the shuttle on a shift like in table tennis double. Further, we play a fixed pattern in the rallies, as the players have to play "cross – cross – straight – cross – cross – straight". The rallies start with a normal serve.

The exercise sounds quite simple, but in my experience, even elite players find this exercise challenging. It is my experience that the players find the exercise fun and motivating.

The demands for reflection are high because of the different premises of the game.

Exercise 59:

This exercise is a progression of exercise 58. Again, we play 2 against 2 on a singles court, and we play "cross – cross – straight" as before.

However, the pair, receiving serve has 1 possibility for each rally to deviate from the pattern. If this opportunity happens, then the rally will be played to the end on the half-court the stroke that deviated from the pattern went.

The demands for reflection in this exercise are very high, especially because of the uncertainty regarding when the shot that deviates from the pattern will be used.

Exercise 60:

This is almost the same exercise as 59. The difference is that in this exercise both pairs can deviate from the pattern.

When a pair deviates from the pattern, the will be played to the end on the half-court, the shot that deviated from the pattern went to.

The demands for reflection are even higher now, compared to exercise 59, as the uncertainty regarding when the deviations will be used are much higher here.

As in all these reflection exercises, it`s a good idea to allow time between rallies for the players to reflect upon how to handle the situation.

Exercise 61:

In this exercise, we play normal doubles – 2 against 2. The rallies start with a short or an offensive long serve. The pair who makes the first defensive shot in the rally, have to stay in defense the rest of the rally.

The exercise looks like a full normal double at the start of the rallies, as the fight for the initiative is part of the modern double.

The exercise demands a lot of reflection from the players as the game changes fundamentally after 1 of the pairs have used a defensive shot. This means, that the players continuously have to reflect upon what to do, depending on if they are in a defensive or offensive position.

In all these exercises, where different rules mean that the game is not like a normal double, it`s very important always to focus on the goal. Off course, we can practice reflective skills, even if the game is not like normal badminton.

Exercise 62:

Again, we play normal doubles 2 against 2. The rallies start with a high, long service to the backline. The pair doing the first offensive shot in the rally have to stay offensive the rest of the rally.

The exercise demands o lot of reflection, as the pair opening the rally with an offensive shot, will be in a bad situation, if the first offensive shot is a bad choice.

As always we allow time between rallies for the players to reflect upon how to handle this exercise, thinking about what happened in the rally before, and what could be the plan for the rallies to come.

Exercise 63:

Normal doubles – 2 against 2. The player in the pair who make the first down-going offensive shot from the backline in the rally is the only player in the pair who can make this kind of shot for the rest of the rally.

The exercise will force the players to reflect upon, which player they prefer at the backline, and try to play the rallies so this player gets the chance to come to the backline.

Exercise 64:

Again, we play normal doubles – 2 against 2. The player in the pair, who plays the pair's first defensive shot, has to play defensive shots the rest of the rally. However, she can kill at the net.

If a pair can play the entire rally without using defensive shots, of course, the pair can play as they want during the rally.

Again, the demands for reflection are very high in this exercise. Especially when a player has been forced to do a defensive shot, the tactics of the game will change dramatically, which probably will increase the risk of mistakes and bad decisions.

Exercise 65:

We play doubles – 2 against 2. The rallies start with an overhand serve, like in tennis. The service will be hit behind the double service line at the back of the court. The server can place herself where she wants at the service line, and the service doesn`t have to be a cross-shot.

As the premise of the game is very different from normal double, the players have to reflect upon how to handle especially the start of the rallies.

In the exercise, we are practising basic reflective skills, as in all the other exercises until now.

Exercise 66:

In this exercise, we play doubles – 2 against 2 on a singles half court. It`s allowed to make a high long service to the single backline.

Again, the demands for reflection are high, as the players have to reflect upon how to handle the change in the fundamental premises of the game.

Like always, we allow time between rallies for the players to reflect upon what has happened and what are their tactics for the next rallies.

2.3 Specific exercises developing "anticipation"

2.3.1 General about the concept of anticipation.

The word "anticipation" comes from the English word "anticipate", which means, "to expect", "to predict" or in other words, when you are good at anticipating, you can look into the future.

When a badminton player is good at anticipating, she is good at predicting what will happen next in a specific rally. In other words, she can look into the future, which is a formulation I use myself, to motivate my players to practice anticipation skills. Who would not want to be able to look into the future?

As mentioned earlier in this book, research from Aalborg University has shown that one of the skills that impart the greatest experience of joy in the game is the skill of anticipation.

Good anticipation skills will in this perspective, create a feeling of joy for the players, and at the same time, good anticipation skills will increase the players` chance of winning the rallies.

The chance of winning badminton matches will in this light increase if the players` can anticipate and react in an appropriate way regarding what they expect will happen next in the rally.

The ability to anticipate can, like everything else be practised. This can be done in exercises that focus on, that the players` being put in situations where there are "clues" which enable them to predict or anticipate what the opponent will do next, and then act regarding what they anticipated.

It's important, that when we practice anticipation, the exercises have to be as functional as possible, which will be explained further a little later in this chapter.

From a learning point of view, the development of anticipation is closely connected to the process of reflection, which means that we from a learning theoretical perspective are working inside the theory of constructivism, as described in chapter 1. This means, that when the player in a specific rally observes the opponent and recognizes the situation from earlier rallies, the player will expect a specific action from the opponent, and therefore prepare to react appropriately. If the opponent how ever does something different from what the player expected, the process of reflection will begin, and the player will analyze the situation, regarding what was different in this situation, compared to what she expected from earlier similar situations. The result of the reflection process hopefully will be, that the player can identify parameters or "clues" which can be recognized next time the situation occurs, which again means that the player has the possibility of anticipating correctly next time.

You can say that anticipative skills are part of the repertoire of competencies that can be developed using reflective basic competencies.

2.3.2 Development of anticipative skills through identification of "clues"

The first basic process regarding the development of reflective skills I call "identification of clues". In other words, this means attention to the signs that can give the player an idea about what the opponent will do next.

When we talk about "clues", being bodily or movement signs indicating what the opponent will do next in the rally, we split these clues up into local/structural clues and global/biological clues.

A focus on local/structural clues means that we gather information from watching single parts of the opponent's body, for example by looking at the racket arm of the opponent, to find out if the position of the arm can reveal what the opponent will do next. Research shows that it`s especially lower-level players who use local/structural clues in their attempt to anticipate on the court.

A focus on global/biological clues means, that you focus on the whole situation, and not only on single parts of it. In praxis, this means, that you focus on the body of the opponent, her position on the court and the opponent`s direction and speed of movement. Research shows, that this approach to the anticipation process is more effective than using local/structural clues, which means that this approach probably will be relevant for most badminton players.

The global/biological approach to the anticipation praxis means, that the exercises as a starting point should be functional and game-like. In specific situations, you could do more formal exercises if the goal of the exercise dictates this.

The process of training anticipative skills demands a lot of work in this area. Research in the area shows that it takes about 6-7 years for a player to develop good anticipative skills, starting from a low level of skills. It is important to know, that the development of anticipative skills only can be done inside the mentioned time interval if the players practice anticipation equally with other technical, tactical and mental competencies.

Regarding elite players` their main challenge regarding anticipating on the court is when the opponent makes deceptions, which of course will happen very often on this level. This means that when we practice anticipative skills with elite players, the exercises should be functional and contain deceptions used by the opponent.

In my experience, players find anticipation practice fun and motivating, and in the following chapter, I will show examples of exercises aiming at developing anticipative skills by identifying clues.

2.3.3 Specific exercises with a focus on identifying clues.

Exercise 67:

In this exercise, we play the normal singles on a singles court. The opponent or the feeder as we often call her has to play short returns on full smashes from the player.

After the smash, the player has to be aware of how much pressure the feeder is under, the more under pressure, the more the chance of a straight smash return. If the feeder is not under too much pressure, she will do a short cross return.

The success criteria in this exercise are that the player can kill the smash return at the net, which of course indicates that she has anticipated correctly. When the player kills at the net after a short smash return from the feeder, she gets 3 points instead of 1.

Examples of clues the players can try to identify are:

- How high a position does the feeder return the smash from – the lower position the more chance of a straight smash return.

- How far away from the body does the feeder return the smash – further away from the body means a bigger chance of a straight smash return.

Exercise 68:

Again, we play a single on a singles court.

The feeder is told always to do a pulled straight forehand or backhand shot from the back line when hitting the shot from a low position. The player doesn`t know which task the feeder has, but she knows that the feeder has been told to do something in specific situations.

The player now has to try to identify clues that can reveal what the feeder has been told to do.

When the player has identified the clue, she will be rewarded the rest of the set, as she can move forward to the net, and make a kill or a spin shot that can be difficult for the feeder to return.

When exercises are done in this way, the players will often identify more clues than the clues the coach has constructed, which means that the exercise will be a general exercise aiming at identifying clues.

Exercise 69:

Normal singles on a singles court. The rule now is, that if the players can decide the rally by making a kill from the net, the players get 3 points instead of 1.

Another rule is, that if a player makes a mistake on purpose to avoid that the opponent can make a kill at the net, the opponent get 3 points. This of course is to avoid that the players will make mistakes on purpose in situations, where their opponent has the chance of making a kill at the net.

The players again have to try to identify clues that will reveal when the opponent is likely to play a shot to the net.

Examples of clues could be:

- If the opponent hits the shot close to the floor at the back line.

- If the opponent hit the shot behind the body at the back line.

- If the opponent is under pressure from a smash, as shown in exercise 67.

- If the opponent hits the shot from a low position at the net.

Exercise 70:

Again, we play normal singles. The only extra rule is, that the players get 3 points instead of 1 if they can catch the shuttle with an overhand catch in front of the service line at the net. I usually tell the players that it is OK to jump into the area and make a catch to get the 3 points.

Again, the players get 3 points if the opponent makes mistakes on purpose.

The exercise is a fantastic anticipation exercise, as it is very difficult so long time in advance to anticipate what the opponent will do, so it will make it possible for the player to catch the shuttle as described.

The clues the players have to be aware of are almost the same as in exercise 69.

Exercise 71:

This exercise is a service and receives exercise for singles.

The player making the serve has to serve towards the middle of the court – meaning towards the "T".

The receiver has to play an offensive shot on the service return, and she has 3 possibilities when returning serve:

- Cross net shot.

- Long flat cross return.

- Long flat straight return.

The players make 5 serves each on shift. If the player serving can play an offensive shot on the service return, she gets 1 point. If the player serving can`t play an offensive shot on the service return, the opponent gets 1 point.

The server has to try to identify the clues that will tell her what return will be used by the receiver.

Examples of clues could be:

- The body position of the receiver.

- The receiver`s choice of shot, for example regarding forehand or backhand shots.

It`s important to underline, that these are only examples as clues can vary depending on the specific opponents you play against.

This exercise is therefore practising the ability to identify specific clues used by specific opponents.

Exercise 72:

This is almost the same exercise as 71. The difference is, that the service doesn`t have to be placed towards the middle. The server can place it where she wants, as long as it is a short serve. Probably this means, that the server can identify more clues regarding what return will be made.

If the service is placed towards the sideline, and the receiver is a little late and hit the shot a little low, the chance of a straight flat long return is big. Often the server will make this service, and afterwards, try to intercept the straight flat return.

Exercise 73:

We play normal singles in this exercise. If the players can make a short or flat cross smash return after a full smash from the opponent, and after this, win the rally without losing the initiative again, the player making the short smash return will get 3 points instead of 1.

The players have to anticipate when the opponent is going to do a full straight smash, and then prepare to return this as an example by moving a little to the side she expects the smash to be placed.

Clues regarding if the opponent will make a straight full smash could be:

- The opponents` placement at the backline. If the opponent is around 1 meter into the court from the backline, the chance of a full smash is big.
- The length of the swing will often reveal if the opponent will do a full smash. The longer swing, the bigger chance of a full smash.
- From the forehand side, the opponent will probably use more straight smashes compared to the backhand side. This is because of the rotation in the forearm. The pronation will make it easier to make a straight smash from the forehand side.

Exercise 74:

As in exercise 73, we play normal singles. If the players in the rally can make a straight short or flat smash return on a full cross smash from the opponent, and after this, win the rally without losing the initiative, the player making the smash return will get 3 points instead of 1.

Again the players have to look for clues telling us when the opponent will do a cross smash.

Clues indicating a cross smash could be:

- The opponent is at the backline on the backhand side of the court.
- The body of the opponent is slightly turned cross.

Exercise 75:

Again, we play normal singles. In this exercise, one of the players is training anticipation, and one of the players is a feeder, who will get some information from the coach about what to do in certain situations.

The player training anticipation knows in advance, what the feeder has to do in the rallies.

Because this exercise among other things is about anticipating as the feeder does deceptions, the exercise is especially relevant for players on a high level, as mentioned at the beginning of this chapter.

When the feeder is at the backline on the forehand side, she has to do a straight delayed clear shot. If the feeder is around 1 meter into the court she can do either a full straight smash or a crosscut shot.

One of the clues is the feeders` placement at the backline. If the feeder is all the way at the backline, the player is standing tall and waiting for the clear shot. If the feeder is a little into the court, the player stands a little lower, waiting for an offensive down going shot.

The clues to be aware of, regarding if the feeder is doing the smash or the cut could be:

- If the feeder is hitting the shot very high, the player might expect a cut shot.

- If the feeder is a little lower, the player could expect a smash.

The feeder has to be told in advance when to do which shot, so the player has a chance of anticipating correctly.

Exercise 76:

Again, we play normal singles. In this exercise, one of the players is training anticipation, and one of the players is a feeder, who will get some information from the coach about what to do in certain situations.

As in exercise 75, the player training anticipation knows in advance, what the feeder has to do in the rallies.

Because this exercise among other things is about anticipating as the feeder does deceptions, the exercise is especially relevant for players on a high level, as mentioned at the beginning of this chapter.

When the feeder is in a good position at the net, she has to make either a backhand spin shot or a delayed cross lob shot.

Clues that could reveal what the feeder will do could be:

- If the feeder hit the shot very high on the net, the probability of a spin shot is high.

- If the feeder hits the shot a little lower, the probability is high.

As in exercise 75, the feeder has to know in advance when to use which shot.

Exercise 77:

I usually call this exercise "play like ……. does", and it is an exercise aimed at training to identify clues.

The players have a couple of days before a training session been asked to choose a player they know either from TV or one of the other players in the specific training group. It is important, that the players selected for this exercise are known by all the players in the training group. However, it is only the individual players, who know the name of the player, they have selected.

The players know have to prepare to be able to play exactly like the player they have selected, by identifying clues that are special for exactly this player.

In the training exercise, the players are playing single against each other, while they have to play like the player selected. After a short set to 5 or 7, the players now have to see if they can identify which player the opponent imitated. If they are not able to do this after the first set, we just play another set and repeat the process after that.

Exercise 78:

This is almost the same exercise as exercise 76. The only difference is, that the coach now decides which players should be copied by the players in the specific training session.

This probably means that the process of identifying clues and copying the selected player will be more challenging than in exercise 76. We can assume that because the players don`t select who they want to copy they will know less about the player, which again will make the process more difficult.

Exercise 79:

This exercise is one of the few exercises in this book, that I didn`t develop myself. I am inspired by the Danish Head coach Kenneth Jonassen, who I have seen use this exercise in the national training centre in Brøndby, Copenhagen.

The exercise is a pure clue identifying exercise. The coach has in advance selected and prepared video sequences with other players, and preferably potential future opponents.

The video sequences show players in situations where they are about to make specific choices in specific situations. The video sequence is stopped just before the player in the video is about to show what she wants to do. The player looking at the video now has to identify clues from the video, that can reveal what the player on the video is about to do. After discussing this with the coach and/or other players, the rest of the video sequence is played and the player can see if she anticipated correctly.

As mentioned, this exercise is good at practice the ability to identify clues and therefore to practice anticipation. At the same time, the exercise will work as a preparation exercise for future opponents.

Exercise 80:

This exercise is an exercise for doubles. The focus is on how to move after doing a short service. In the exercise, the players are working together 2 and 2.

The exercise starts up with a short service to the middle of the court, meaning against the "cross". 4 players can be on 1 court at the same time doing the exercise because we are only focusing on the movement of the server in this exercise.

The receiver in the exercise has been told to do either an overhand return or an underhand return.

The player serving must be aware of the position of the receiver's racket at the moment she is receiving the service because in this exercise the racket position is the clue. If the receiver makes an overhand return, the server is staying in the position she served from, anticipating a pushed return of 1 to 2 meters long. If the receiver makes an underhand return, the server moves towards the net, because the receiver often will make a shot to the net from this position.

Exercise 81:

In this exercise, we play a normal double. The players will get 3 points instead of 1 if the net player can finish the rally from the net after her partner has made a smash from the backline.

The net player has to be aware of the quality of the smash from the partner, both regarding speed and placement. Also, the net player has to try to identify clues telling her how much under pressure the opponents are when trying to return the smash. The more under pressure the opponents are, the more the probability for a straight, short return.

Clues that could reveal if the opponents are under pressure returning the smash:

Exercise 82:

Again in this exercise, we play a normal double. If the pair can make a flat contra return on a smash from the opponents, and hereafter win the rally without giving away the initiative, they get 3 points instead of 1.

As a basic rule, the players should do a flat cross return on straight smashes, and a straight flat return on cross smashes. In specific situations, the players can deviate from this rule.

The pair being in a defensive position have to look for clues that reveal if they get a chance to do a contra shot.

Clues in this exercise could for example be:

- The player making the smash is not in an optimal position, for example, hitting the shot from a low position.

- The player making the smash is moving sideways while doing the smash.

As I have mentioned before, these clues are only examples. Specific opponents and specific situations will mean that different clues could be identified.

The anticipation exercises in this book are primarily aimed at developing general anticipation skills that enable the players to identify both specific and general clues.

2.3.4 Development of anticipative skills by "recognition of patterns"

The second basic process regarding the development of reflective skills, I call "recognition of patterns".

In this process, you don't look for clues from the opponents' body, placement and so on. Instead, the focus is on trying to identify habits or patterns in the way the opponent is playing. In other words, you focus on if the opponent in specific situations has a tendency to do the same things. For example, can the opponent have a tendency to always make a cross smash when she is placed at the backline on the backhand side of the court.

Clues from the body are in this situation less important than the fact, that the opponent does these patterns, which you can anticipate and gain an advantage. I will argue that habits and patterns of play are more relevant on a lower level. At an elite level, the opponent probably will find out about this very fast, and take advantage of it.

However, there can be general patterns, which are relevant to play even at an elite level. For example, you will often intercept a flat cross clear from the opponent with a straight stick smash. In this situation, the player will be in a good position where the fixed pattern is the best solution no matter if the opponent knows what the player will do.

In the following, I will describe examples of exercises aiming at being able to register habits and patterns from the opponent.

2.3.5 Specific anticipation exercises with a focus on the identification of habits and patterns.

Exercise 83:

In this exercise, we play singles on a singles court and one of the players is practising anticipating patterns at the opponent. The other player is a feeder, and this player will before the match start, pick a playing card from a pile of cards beside the court.

A red card means that the feeder shall always make shorts services towards the sideline. A black card means that the feeder shall always play a cross-cut shot from the deep forehand side when she is in a position to do an overhand shot.

The player practising anticipation doesn`t know what the feeder has to do in the match.

The player has to identify the pattern as fast as possible, so she can take advantage of this for the rest of the set.

We play shorts sets to for example 7 points, and it is a good idea to play 2 – 3 sets with the same task for the feeder. We play short sets because the set doesn`t have to go on much longer after the player has identified the task of the feeder. The optimal situation is, that the set goes on 2 or 3 rallies after the player has identified the pattern, so the player can benefit from anticipating correctly.

Depending on the level of the players, you can make the sets longer or shorter.

Exercise 84:

This exercise is almost the same as exercise 83. The difference is that both players pick a card before the set starts.

The players get different tasks. For example, for player A, a red card means she shall always make short services, and for player B a red card means she shall always make lob shots from the net. A black card means that player A shall always make net drops from the net, and a black card means that player B shall always make a cross smash from the backline at the backhand side of the court.

The players don't know what the tasks of the opponent are.

Again we play short sets to 7, and it's a good idea to play 3-4 sets with the same tasks. The players pick a new card between each set.

Exercises 83 and 84 can vary in many different ways, depending on which tasks the cards define.

Exercise 85:

Again, we are playing singles on a singles court. In the exercise, we have a player who practices identifying patterns in the opponent's game and a feeder who has a task to do.

For example, the feeder is told never to do cross lob shots in the rallies.

The player shall try to identify the task with the purpose of anticipating and getting an advantage in the rallies.

Again, we play short sets to 7 points.

This exercise is more challenging than exercise 84 because the task of the feeder is more difficult to identify.

This exercise again can be varied in many ways, as there are a lot of shots which can be removed from the feeders' game.

Exercise 86:

Same exercise as exercise 85 except in this exercise both players get a task in the sets. For example one of the players can`t make a straight net drop in the rallies, while the other player can`t make a cross net drop.

Again, we play short sets to 7 points.

The exercise probably is a little more challenging compared to exercise 85, as both players now have to try to identify the opponents` task, and at the same time remember to play according to their own task.

Again, this exercise can vary in many ways, as the number of different tasks possible is very high.

Exercise 87:

This is a 2 against 1 exercise. The players playing together are feeders for the player who is alone.

The task of the 2 players is always to make short smash returns. When the player has identified this task, she can take advantage of this, because she can anticipate the short smash return and follow up on the net to make a kill.

As in previous exercises, we play short sets of 5 or 7 points depending on how fast the player identifies the feeders` task.

Again, the exercises can vary in many ways depending on the feeders' task.

Exercise 88:

This exercise is almost the same as exercise 87. The difference is that the feeders get a task each.

For example, can one of the feeders only make long smash returns, while the other feeder can`t make net drops.

The exercise probably is a little more challenging than exercise 87, because the player now has to identify 2 tasks to gain full advantage.

Again, we play short sets. However, in this exercise, the sets probably have to be a little longer, so the player has the chance of identifying both tasks.

As in previous exercises, this exercise can vary in many ways depending on the task of the feeders.

Exercise 89:

This is a 2 against 2 playing on a doubles court. We play normal double except that the players in one of the pairs have a task to do. For example, they shall always make cross smash returns.

The other pair has free play, and their task is to identify the task of the feeders, so they can take advantage of this for the rest of the set.

When the task has been identified, the pair who has free play for example can change their position when attacking so that the net player will move to the other side of the court than her partner, as she knows the feeders will make a cross smash return.

As always in these exercises, the length of the set is adjusted to the level of the players. The players have to have time to identify the task of the feeders, and also have time to benefit from this in the last rallies in the set. Probably the sets should be shorter the higher the level of the players is.

As mentioned before, this exercise can vary in many ways depending on the task of the feeders.

Exercise 90:

This exercise is almost the same as exercise 89. The difference is that both pairs now have a task to do. For example, one of the pairs always should do service returns short or just around the server, while the other pair always has to make long smash returns.

As exercise 89, this exercise can vary in many ways depending on the tasks of the players.

As in the previous exercises, we play short sets. Probably the sets have to be a little longer if the level is low. The idea is that the players have enough time to identify the tasks and benefit from this knowledge afterwards, as it enables them to anticipate and win the rally.

Exercise 91:

This exercise is a progression from exercise 90, as all 4 players now have a task.

The exercise is more challenging because the players have fewer opportunities to identify the tasks.

Probably the sets have to be a little longer than in exercise 90.

Again, the exercise can vary in many ways depending on the tasks of the players.

2.3.6 Development of anticipative skills doing "split vision" practice.

An important element regarding the development of anticipation skills is what we can call "the peripheral field of view". When we look at the world, we use first our primary field of view. This means the area in our field of view where our focus is, and where the things we see are sharp and focused. This way we register and can act according to what we see.

However, the primary field of view is not especially broad. If you stretch out the arm in front of you and turn the thump vertically upwards, and then lay down the thump to a horizontal position to the right and left, the distance from thump tip to thump tip will be the width of our primary field of view.

The primary field of view of course is the most important field of view when we play badminton. If you have tried to hit the shuttle without looking directly at it, you know how difficult this is.

However, apart from the primary field of view we also have what we call the "peripheral field of view". This field of view is very broad, up to 190 degrees, which enables us to register movements a little behind us. The ability to use our peripheral field of view is very important when we play badminton because it enables us before we hit the shuttle, to register where on-court our opponent is, and even more important which direction she is headed. This information is an important clue regarding what the opponent plans to do in the rally, and therefore a clue that enables the player to anticipate and choose appropriate solutions.

In this book, I choose to understand the peripheral field of view not only as a view that registers horizontal to the sides but as a 180-degree field of view that enables us to register vertical movement as well as horizontal movement, and also movements in front of what is focused on with the primary field of view. This means that we can register movements at the same time we focus on the shuttle in the primary field of view.

This ability is as indicated important regarding being able to anticipate and make relevant solutions in badminton matches.

Research shows that the peripheral field of view can be expanded and improved through practice. In the following, I will describe several more or less functional exercises, aiming at developing the peripheral field of view, and thus developing the players' ability to anticipate and make relevant choices in the match.

I call these exercises "split vision" exercises, as the title indicates that you have to be able to look at several things at the same time. In other words, you have to be able to "split" up your vision.

2.3.7 specific exercises training "split vision"

Exercise 92

In this exercise, the coach is standing at the sideline with one leg on each side of the net post. The players are working together 2 and 2, as 1 of the players is a feeder and throws shuttles to the net.

The player training split vision has to make either a backhand net drop or a backhand cross lob shot when returning the shuttle from the feeder.

As mentioned, the coach is standing at the sideline, with his arms down the side of the body. Just before the player receives the shuttle, the coach raises either the left or the right arm to a horizontal position. If the right arm is raised the player has to do a net drop. If the left arm is raised the player has to do a cross lob shot.

The player has to be able to look at the shuttle and at the same time, from the corner of her eye, register which arms the coach is raising.

The exercise should be done so the player has the coach on her left side, to be able to do the shots in the right way. If the player has to do forehand shots, the coach will be placed to the right of the player.

The described exercise is for right-handed players. For left-handed players of course it is the other way around.

Exercise 93:

This exercise is a progression from exercise 92.

The player now has 3 options for returning the shuttle. She can play straight net drop, cross net drop or cross lob shot.

The coach now has 3 signals telling the player what option to choose.

If the coach, as in exercise 92 raise either his right or left arm to a horizontal position, the player again has to do either a straight net drop or a cross lob shot. If the coach raises both arms to a horizontal position, the player has to do a cross-net drop.

This exercise is more complicated than exercise 92 because the player now has to be able to register 3 signals from the coach.

Exercise 94:

In this exercise, the players again are working together 2 and 2.

The players are placed on both sides of the net and in front of each other. One of the players will be a feeder, and her task is to throw a shuttle to the net as in the exercise before. The other task for the feeder in this exercise is that she has to show the player what to do by moving either forwards or backwards just after throwing the shuttle.

If the feeder takes a little step forward just after throwing the shuttle, the player has to do a cross lob shot. If the feeder takes a little step backwards, the player has to do a straight net drop. The exercise should be done on the player's backhand side.

This exercise is more functional than exercise 93, as the situation is much more game-like.

The exercise trains the peripheral field of view directly in front of what we focus on with the primary field of view, which is an important competence, especially when both players in the match are close to the net.

You can do either backhand or forehand shots in this exercise, depending on which side of the court the exercise is done.

Exercise 95:

The exercise is a progression from exercise 94.

Again, the feeder throws a shuttle to the, with the player standing in front of the feeder on the other side of the net.

The feeder now has 3 signals telling the player what to do. If the feeder, as in exercise 94, moves either forward or backwards after throwing the shuttle, the player again has to do either a cross lob shot or a straight net drop. If the feeder stands still after throwing the shuttle, the player has to do a cross-net drop.

The exercise is a little more challenging compared to exercise 94 because the player now has to register 3 signals instead of 2 through the peripheral field of view.

Again the player can do either backhand or forehand shots depending on which side of the court you are.

Exercise 96:

Again, in this exercise, we have a feeder and a player training split vision.

The feeder makes a high service to the backline. The player has to do either a straight or a cross smash. Just before the player hits the shuttle, the feeder moves a little to one or the other side of the court.

The player now has to focus on the shuttle and at the same time try to register in the peripheral field of view, to which side the feeder is moving. If the player registers the feeders` movement correctly, the smash should be hit to the other side from where the feeder is moving.

In this exercise, it is a good idea to tell the player not to lower the head and look directly at the feeder, as this will mean we are not training split vision anymore.

Exercise 97:

This exercise is a progression from exercise 96.

Again, we have a feeder doing a long service to the backline and a player who has to return the service according to a signal from the feeder.

After the service and just before the player is about to return the shuttle, the feeder makes a directional pre-loading jump. If the feeder for example stands with her right foot in front of the left after the preloading jump, it means that the feeder easily can move in the direction the line between the feet is pointing.

The player has to try to register the direction of the pre-loading jump, and then return the shuttle to 1 of the 2 corners the feeder is not covering.

Exercise 98:

In this exercise, the feeder makes a short service and then turns the pre-loading jump, either with the right foot in front or the left foot in front.

If the feeder has the right foot in front it indicates, that she after making the service, wants to move towards the net, which means that the player has to make a return to the backline. If the feeder has the left foot in front it indicates, that she wants to move backwards after making the service, which is why the player has to do a short return.

If the player is left-handed, the exercise is the other way around.

Exercise 99:

In this exercise, we have 2 feeders and a player training split vision. The shuttle has to be played to 1 of the 4 corners, both by the feeders and the player.

The feeders have to hit the shuttle on shift. The player has to try to register in which corner the feeder who will make the next shot is placed. The feeder who has to do the next shot will be standing in the middle of the court, and move to 1 of the corners just before the player will hit the shuttle to her.

The exercise takes a little habituation, especially regarding the feeders, who have to move so late that the player doesn`t have time to look directly at them before doing the shots. On the other hand, the feeders have to move early enough for the player to register their movements using the peripheral field of view.

Depending on the level of the players, the feeders have to move a little earlier or a little later before the player has to make the shot.

Exercise 100:

This exercise is a progression from exercise 99.

Again, we have 2 feeders and a player who practices split vision. The feeders now can choose to move to the 6 places as shown in figure 14.

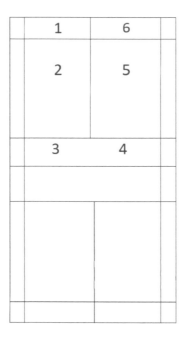

Figure 14.

When the feeders move to areas 2 and 5, the player has to attack with a smash. The feeders should only play to areas 2 and 5 when the player is in a good position at the backline.

Because of the extra 2 areas compared to exercise 99, the exercise is more challenging, both for the feeders and for the player.

Exercise 101:

In this exercise, we play a singles match in short sets of 5 or 7 seven points.

Both players are told to "take chances" in the rallies, meaning that they have to move in good time before the opponent hits the shuttle.

In this way, the players will have plenty of opportunities to register movements through the peripheral field of view.

When we do exercises like this it`s important that the players are not focused on winning or losing, but instead try to help each other with training split vision by moving around the court in the right way.

CHAPTER 3

Exercises with a social learning perspective

3.1. A little about social learning theory

Social learning theory sees learning as a social phenomenon, which means, that learning takes place between people in social relations. In this perspective, learning takes place when people are together in groups, and learn from talking to each other and observing each other in different situations. The ability to communicate in relevant ways is thus an important competence regarding social learning.

Also, social learning theory sees learning as being "situated". This means that when you are in social connections, for example, at a badminton practice or in a school class, you learn what is relevant to be able to handle the demands in a specific context. Because learning in a badminton practice is situated, the players in the practice learn to play badminton, to participate according to the framework of the practice, and so on.

It`s important to understand, that there is no contradiction between understanding learning from an individual and constructivist perspective, and understanding learning as a social phenomenon, as I do in this section. The different learning approaches are supplementing each other, and the way learning specifically takes place depends on the context we are part of. Social learning theory does not dispute that we reflect when we experience new and unexpected things and that the reflection process is important in order to learn in general. Social learning theory only states, that no matter what it is in social relations we get the inputs and disturbances that are a condition for the reflection process to take place, as described in chapter 2.

Swiss learning theorist Etienne Wenger together with his colleague American anthropologist Jean Lave are the scientists who have developed social learning theory. Their definition of what social learning is tells us that learning is "social participation". As indicated above, we learn when we are together with other people dealing with something of common interest. This learning context automatically will create a feeling of "relatedness" among the players, which, as mentioned before, is an important condition for becoming intrinsically motivated.

In this book, I will split the social learning process up into 2 different specific contexts. The first situation is what Wenger calls learning in "a community of practice". The second situation is learning in what I call a "team".

The 2 different learning contexts can contribute to developing different competencies for the players, competencies that can help increase the experience of fun in the game, as well as improve players` level of play.

3.1.2. What characterizes specific exercises with a social learning theoretical approach?

The following specific parameters will in general characterize exercises with a social learning approach.

- The players work together in groups of a minimum of 3 participants.
- In the exercises, there shall be breaks and time for communication between the players, so the players can develop good solutions regarding the specific tasks they are dealing with.
- The players in the group are depending on each other because all members of the group have to succeed for the

whole group to succeed.
- The best and most experienced players shall often have the possibility for and the motivation to help less experienced players. This is especially important when we are working in "communities of practice".

In the following section, I will briefly describe what a community of practice is, and after that present specific exercises inside this area.

3.2 Learning in communities of practice

As mentioned earlier Wenger says that learning is taking place in communities of practice, where the participants learn from each other and also to each other. A community of practice is in this way a group of people who participates in a common activity, for example, badminton, an activity all members of the community find important to engage in. Communities of practice are characterized by having a common language that creates a feeling of relatedness for the members of the community. An example of such a common language would be when a handball team call their game systems by secret names. The battle cry that many badminton teams do before matches is another example of such a common language.

As mentioned the members of a community of practice engage in the same activities, but they participate with different levels of skills. You can argue, that normal training in a badminton club could be defined as a community of practice because all the players engage in the same activity, but some players probably are better than other players. We say that the players have "overlapping" competencies, which means that the players should be able to do the same things but some are on a higher level than others.

This difference in level between the players in the community of practice creates the possibility for the coach to do exercises, where better players can function as teachers and role models for players with a lower level of skills.

Exercises with this perspective have the potential to develop several important competencies for the players. Primarily the exercises can develop communicative skills because the exercises, as I will describe later, invite the players to talk and discuss in groups, to be able to handle the tasks given to them. Communicative skills of course are important if the players should be able to learn from each other, which is the second important aim of doing community of practice exercises.

These kinds of exercises will focus on the community as an important condition for learning, and thus will create understanding regarding that we need each other to optimize the learning context.

In the next section, I will present a number of exercises taking place in the communities of practice.

3.3. Specific exercises based on communities of practice.

Exercise 102:

In this exercise, 2 teams are competing against each other. The players on the same team are together 2 and 2 on a singles half court. The exercise is "lob – drop – backhand spin shot – lob" and so on. If the exercise stops, we start up again with a high service to the backline. The goal of the exercise is to hit the top of the net tape with the backhand spin shot. All players on the team have to hit the top of the net 3 times for the team to finish and win the competition.

As the technical demands are the same for all players in this exercise, we can assume that the better players hit the top of the net 3 times in less time than the lower-level players do. When players have hit the top of the net 3 times they are encouraged to help and coach the players on the team, that have not finished yet.

The better players will be motivated to help the other players, as the team can only win the competition if all players succeed.

In this way, the exercise will develop communicative skills, and at the same time develop an understanding that it is possible to learn from and also to each other.

Exercise 103:

This exercise is a progression from exercise 102.

The difference is, that the players can decide for themselves if they want to use a backhand or a forehand spin shot to try to hit the top of the net.

The task for the players who finish early is to coach and guide the other players regarding both technical issues and advice regarding what kind of spin shot to use, taking into consideration the specific player`s level of competence.

These kinds of exercises for sure will help to create a training environment based on respect for each other, and understanding, that you can become better by helping each other

Exercise 104:

This exercise is a variation from exercises 102 and 103. Again, we have 2 teams competing against each other, as the players are together 2 and 2 on the specific team.

One of the players in the pair makes a high service to the backline, and the partner has to try to hit the shuttle with the frame of the racket. The shot will count if the shuttle is hit with the frame no matter if the shuttle passes the net.

When all the players on the team have done 1 shot with the frame, the competition is finished and the team win the match.

It's a good idea to do the exercise 3 – 5 times, so the teams can discuss how a relevant technique could be to be able to hit the shuttle with the frame of the racket.

The exercise again develops communicative competencies. Further, the exercise creates the possibility that the players who are best at this specific discipline can help the other players. With a little bit of luck, players that are not in normal situations the best players can succeed in this exercise, and experience that they can help the other players, and become recognized for this.

Exercise 105:

In this exercise, 2 teams are playing a match against each other, and we play singles on a half or a full court, depending on the number of courts and players. The teams are put up in order of strength, an order made by the teams themselves before the exercise starts. The highest ranking player of one team is playing against the highest ranking player on the other team and so on.

We play for example for 15 minutes, and the team with the most points after the period win the match.

Before the match, the teams are told by the coach that there is a restriction on the single game. For example, you can only use 1 lob shot at each rally.

Before the match starts, the teams will have 2 minutes to discuss what tactical consequences the restriction will have for the game.

After half of the match time has passed, there will be a little break, where the teams can discuss and evaluate tactics. These small breaks for communication will be an opportunity for the better players to help and coach the other players on the team. The players should be motivated for helping each other, as the team can only win the match if all players contribute with points.

The exercise can variate in many ways depending on the specific restriction of the game.

Exercise 106:

In the exercise, we play "around the court", which is a well-known and loved exercise in badminton practice, and again it`s a team competition.

We have 6 – 8 players on each team, and the teams are playing the exercise on one court, with an equal number of players on each side of the net at the start of the exercise. When a player has hit the shuttle, she runs around the court to the other side and stands at the back of the row on the other side of the net.

The first team that can`t return the shuttle loses the match.

In the exercise, the players can choose for themselves how they want to return the shuttle.

Before the exercise starts, the teams have a couple of minutes to how they can handle the exercise. For example, it could be relevant to discuss which players are standing where in the rows. Also, it could be relevant to discuss where to place the returns so teammates will have a good position for their next shots. The aim of the exercise is, that better players or players with experience in this specific exercise take control and lead the discussions in the team.

The exercise can be done 3 – 4 times so the teams have the opportunity to discuss how the exercise should be handled. In this way, the exercise develops communicative skills and encourages experienced players to help less experienced players.

The exercise, as described here, probably aims at lower-level players, because the free shot selection makes the exercise very easy for higher levels of players.

Exercise 107:

This exercise is a progression from exercise 106.

Again we play "around the court" in team competition as described in exercise 106. In this exercise, we have 6 players on each team. The teams are playing the exercise on one court, with an equal number of players on each side of the net at the start of the exercise. When a player has hit the shuttle, she runs around the court to the other side and stands at the back of the row on the other side of the net.

From one side of the court, the players have to make a clear shot no longer than the double service line at the back. From the other side of the court, the players have to make a smash. Not necessarily a full smash, but just a down-going shot.

The first team that can`t return the shuttle loses the match.

Before the exercise, the teams have a couple of minutes to discuss how to handle this exercise. Again the aim of the exercise is, that more experienced players help less experienced players, and through this process, the exercise helps develop communicative skills for all the players in the team.

This exercise is much more demanding compared to exercise 106 and can be done with high-level players.

Exercise 108:

This exercise is a variation from the traditional "round the court" game. We have for example 12 players available for the exercise. These 12 players are placed on 5 courts, so they are standing 2 and 2 in front of each other on a half court. The last 2 players are standing at the net posts at courts 1 and 5.

The exercise starts with the players on one side of the court making a high service to the other side of the court, and after this move half a court to the right. The players on the opposite half return the service with a straight clear shot and move half a court right. After this, the players make straight clear shots and move half a court right for the rest of the exercise. The 2 players standing at the net-posts on courts 1 and 5 move into the court when the player standing on the court moves half a court to the right. The players moving to the right from the right side of court 1 or 5, moves to the position at the net-post.

I usually do this exercise as a competition between the coach and the players. Before the exercise, the coach and the players discuss and agrees on how long time the players shall keep the exercise going to win the competition against the coach. For example, the goal for the players is to keep the exercise going for 45 seconds before a shuttle drops on the floor on one of the five courts. When you have done the exercise a couple of times, you will have a good idea of, how long time it is realistic for the players to keep the exercise going.

The exercise should be done 3 – 4 times, and the goal regarding how long time the exercise should run can be adjusted, so the players don't win the competition against the coach in the first couple of attempts. Between the attempts, the players will have the possibility to discuss how they can handle the exercise to win the competition against the coach. The breaks between the attempts give the more experienced players the possibility to help and coach less experienced players. The optimal situation is, that the players can keep the exercise going longer than the agreed time after 2 or 3 attempts, as this will indicate that the discussions in the team have been constructive.

I will suggest that this exercise is done with players of a good level, as the demands for technical skills are quite high.

Exercise 109

This exercise is a progression from exercise 108.

The difference is that the players on one side of the net are doing straight clear shots, while the players on the other side of the net are doing smashes. It doesn't have to be a full smash, but just a down-going shot.

This exercise is a lot more demanding compared to exercise 108 because the players now have to take into consideration both the length and speed of the clear shots and try to coordinate this with the speed of the smashes.

It can be necessary to have maybe 14 players for 5 courts in exercise so there will be 2 players standing at net posts on courts 1 and 5. This will give the players a little more time to return the shuttle and move half a court right.

I suggest that this exercise is done with really good players, and it`s not often that my players have been able to keep the exercise going for more than 60 seconds.

Again the exercise should be done 3 – 5 times, so the players have time between the attempts to help each other and discuss tactics for the next attempts.

The optimal situation is if the players succeed at the last attempt by reaching for example 50 seconds without dropping a shuttle.

Exercise 110:

This Exercise is primarily aimed at developing communicative skills.

We have 2 teams competing against each other, as we play half-court singles on a number of courts. The teams can consist of 8 – 12 players depending on the number of courts and players available. Before the exercise starts, the teams have to put up their singles in order of strength. In the exercise player 1 from one team always play half-court single against player 1 from the other team. Player 2 against player 2 and so on. One of the teams is placed on the same side of the court, and the other team is placed on the other side.

Each team get 13 playing cards, for example, the 13 harts. The cards have to be mixed and put on the floor behind one of the courts on the same side the specific team is, with the backside upwards. In the exercise, we play short single matches for 2 or 3 points, and the winner of a match can run to the cards behind the team's courts and turn 1 card to see what value it has. The task for the team is to turn all 13 cards in order from 1 to 13, or from ace to king. If the first card the player turns is a 6, the card is put down with the backside upwards. When a player turns the ace, the card is put back with the image side upwards, and the team now has to find card number 2. I usually tell the players that they can only stand at the cards for 3 seconds, so they can't wait at the cards to pass on information to their teammates that also have won a match. This forces the teams to discuss how they can pass on information from the courts to the players who have to turn the next cards. When one of the teams has turned all 13 cards, the team wins the competition.

It is the old children's game "memory" we play in this exercise.

Before the exercise starts, the teams, apart from defining the order of strength, also discuss how they can place the cards on the floor, and how they can organize the communication. I normally tell the players, that the cards must be placed inside a square meter on the floor in an optional pattern. This pattern must be maintained, no matter if the cards have the image side or the neutral upwards.

It is a good idea to do this exercise 2 or 3 times, so the teams can discuss tactics and improve from game to game.

Exercise 111:

This exercise is a variation from exercise 110.

Again, we play 2 teams against each other, as we play half-court singles to 2 or 3 points. Each team has a full deck of cards lying behind their courts with the neutral side upwards. Every time a player on the team wins a match, the player can turn a card from the deck. The card turned will now, for the rest of the game have the image side upwards.

The exercise is a poker game with modified rules. The team has to turn counting combinations as in real poker. The combinations that count in this game are:

· 1 pair

· 2 pair

· 3 alike

· Full house (3 x 2 alike)

· A straight (5 cards in a row, for example, 2-6, but not necessarily the same color. If both teams have a straight, the straight with the highest number wins)

During the game, the teams have to decide when they want to stop the game, as the game can only stop when a team has a counting combination.

The teams must not know what combinations the opponent has turned. For example, a team can stop the game having turned a pair, and then find out that the other team already has turned 3 alike.

The exercise should be repeated several times so the players have the opportunity to discuss tactics for the next game. Of course, the cards are mixed between each game.

The exercise is fun and develops communicative competencies, and the ability to learn from each other and also to each other. The element of competition will increase the intensity of the exercise, as competitions always do.

Exercise 112:

This exercise is again a team competition between 2 teams. We play singles on a half or a full court depending on the number of players. The coach makes the teams so they are as equal as possible.

The teams now define an order of strength, so the best player on one team play against the best player on the other team and so on. The players in this way know before the exercise starts, who will be their opponent in the match.

Depending on the number of players on each team, the teams have to have a number of points, which is the maximum number the team can get in the match. For example, a team with 8 players can get a maximum of 160 points. The 160 points are distributed among the 8 players with the little twist that each player shall have a minimum of 10 points. The points each player gets will be the number of points she has to win, to win the match against her opponent. If a player has to win 10 points to win her match and only gets 7 points before the opponent has reached her number of points, the player will contribute 7 points to the total score of the team. The team with the highest total number of points is the winner.

Because the players know who their opponents are before the match, the teams have to discuss how the points shall be distributed between the players to get the highest total score.

As before it`s a good idea to do the exercise 2-3 times so the teams will have the opportunity to discuss tactics between the games.

The exercise is fun and develops communicative skills.

Exercise 113:

The exercise is a variation from exercise 112, but opposite to that exercise, we now play doubles. The 2 teams shall rank their doubles in order of strength, without the 2 best players necessary having to play together in the 1. Double.

The teams now have to discuss how many points the constellations have to win, and also discuss how to put together and rank the constellations, to get the best chance of winning the competition.

The total number of points the teams can score as a maximum, of course, depends on the number of doubles on each team, as on the time available.

As in exercise 112, it`s a good idea to define a minimum number of points the pairs have to win, so we avoid finishing too early and wasting too much practice time.

The exercise is more challenging regarding demands for communicative skills compared to exercise 11[i]2 because the players now have to relate to more parameters during their negotiations in the group. Also, the exercise creates the possibility that better players pair up with lower-level players, which increases the possibility for players to learn from each other.

Exercise 114:

In this exercise, we play 3 against 3 using table tennis rules. This means, that the players have to hit the shuttle on shift. We play short sets to 3 points on a normal singles court.

Optimally we play 3 – 5 sets, as this will allow the players to discuss tactics between the sets.

To increase the possibility of creating situations where more experienced players can help less experienced players the groups should be heterogeneous, meaning some players are better than others in the group.

Depending on the level of the players, you can play a free game with high-level players, and for example, without smashes for lower-level players.

Exercise 115:

This exercise is a progression from exercise 114. Again, we play 3 against 3, and the players have to hit the shuttle on shift. However, the players only have 2 rackets available which means, that they have to hand the racket to one of the other players after having hit the shuttle. Again, we play short sets to 3 or 5, which gives the players the opportunity to discuss tactics between the sets.

Development of communicative skills and internal learning between the players are the goals of the exercise.

Exercise 116:

The exercise is a variation from exercise 115.

Again, we play 3 against 3 on a singles court, and the players have to hit the shuttle on shift.

The rally starts with a high service to the backline, and the receiving side now has to touch the shuttle 6 times. The 6. time they touch the shuttle it shall be returned to the other side.

Each of the 3 players has to touch the shuttle 2 times after each other, first with the body (but not the hand or the arm), and then with the racket. The sequence in the then is body, racket, body, racket, body, racket. The last touch with the racket shall as mentioned, return the shuttle to the other side.

The groups have to change the order the players hit the shuttle in between each rally.

Again, it`s a good idea to play short sets, so the players can discuss technical and tactical issues between the sets.

Depending on the level of the players, the exercise can be made harder just by starting the sequence with a touch by the racket instead of touch with the body.

Exercise 117:

In this exercise, we play 3 against 3 and the players have to hit the shuttle in a fixed order in the specific set. We play on a normal singles court.

In the exercise, it's only allowed to do 4 shots, being shots to the 4 corners of the court. In other words, the players can only do clear or drop shots.

The players on the same side of the net can never play 2 shots in a row to the same corner.

Before the exercise, the 2 teams discuss how the initial tactics should be. They have to decide the order in which the players hit the shuttle, and where to place themselves on the court, to make the exercise work.

We play short sets for example to 5 points, so the players have the opportunity to discuss and evaluate tactics between the sets.

At the start of a new set, the players can change the order in which they hit the shots.

Exercise 118:

The exercise is a progression from exercise 117. Again, we have 3 players on each team who should hit the shuttle on a shift in a fixed order. The players can only hit to the 4 corners as in exercise 117.

The difference now is, that the players only have 2 rackets available. The players thus have to hand the rackets on to their partners after hitting the shuttle.

The exercise is more challenging compared to exercise 117, as the players now have to change rackets, and at the same time remember which corner they can't play.

Again, we play short sets so the players can discuss tactics between the sets.

It can be a good idea, that the coach makes heterogeneous groups so the more experienced players can help the less experienced players.

Exercise 119:

The exercise is a further progression from exercises 117 and 118. We play on a singles court, and the 3 players now again have one racket each and have to hit the shuttle on a shift in a fixed order. As in the previous exercises, we can`t play in the same area on the court 2 times in a row.

The players now can return to 6 areas as shown in figure 15.

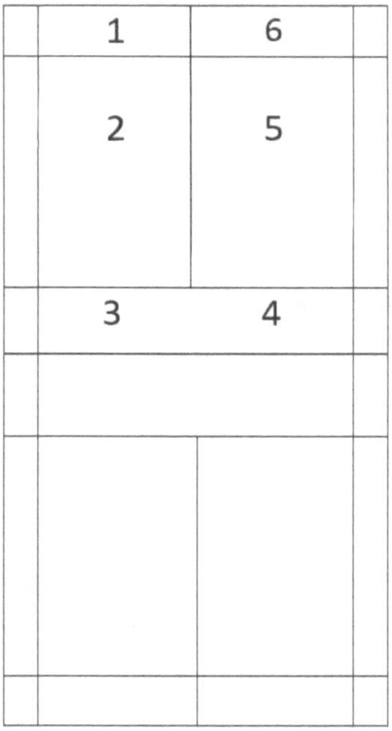

Figure 15.

Areas 2 and 5 indicate that the players can do smashes to these areas.

The exercise is very challenging because the players now have 6 areas to relate to during the game.

We play short sets, so the players can discuss and make plans between the sets.

Again, the coach makes heterogeneous groups, so the experienced players can help the less experienced players.

Exercise 120:

The exercise is a progression from exercise 119. The only difference is, that the players now have only 2 rackets available. The player who just hit the shuttle has to give the racket to one of her partners.

The exercise is very challenging, and the demands for communication between the players are very high.

Again, we work with heterogeneous groups, so the exercises facilitate the social learning perspective.

Exercise 121:

In this exercise, the players are together 4 and 4, and all the players in the team are placed on the same court, with 2 on each side of the net.

The task of the team is to keep as many shuttles as possible in the air at the same time. The teams can organize the exercise as they want, as long as there are 2 players on each side of the net.

The exercise is done on time, for example, 2 minutes, after which the team who had the most shuttles in the air at the same time won.

The exercise should be done a number of times so the teams have the possibility to handle the exercise. Again, we make heterogeneous teams to facilitate internal learning in the group.

Exercise 122:

In this exercise, 2 teams are playing against each other using the full singles court or singles half court depending on the number of players and courts.

The coach makes the teams, so they are as equal as possible.

The teams define for themselves an order of strength, thus the strongest player on one team will play against the strongest player on the other team and so on.

If we, for example, have 5 players on each team, and we have 5 courts available, we play 5 singles on a full singles court. On the 5 courts, we have 5 different restrictions. These could for example be:

- Court 1 – normal singles.
- Court 2 – The court consists of the back and front ditches.
- Court 3 – Box play = the area between the doubles service lines.
- Court 4 - The players can only do 1 backhand shot every rally.
- Court 5 – The players can only do underhand shots.

We play short matches on time, for example, 5 minutes. After each match, they rotate, so the pairs playing against each other play on a court with a new restriction. We do 5 rotations so all players will play all the restrictions.

Between matches, the team should have time to discuss and coach each other regarding the different restrictions.

The team who in the end has won the most matches is the winner of the competition.

The exercise can vary in many ways depending on what restrictions we play on the courts.

3.4 Learning and practising in "teams".

The following specific exercises are examples of, how you can work with a team approach in badminton training, as this approach has the potential to develop important competencies, that can be useful regarding the players' experience of fun, as well as working with team exercises will have the potential to improve the level of play for the players.

When we work in teams, we are still in a social learning context. As described earlier, this means that we learn to each other and also from each other, when we participate in different groups. The specific group, in this case, is called a "team".

As described earlier, a community of praxis is characterized by that the participants should be able to do the same things, or in other words have the same competencies, only on different levels of skills. For example, all the players have to have basic technical skills to be able to function on the level of the specific group. In this perspective, some players are better than others and thus can help other players, while lower-level players receive help.

A team is defined almost in the opposite way from a community of praxis, regarding the competencies of the players. Where, a community of praxis is defined, by the players having the same overlapping competencies, a team is defined by the players having different and complementary competencies. In other words, the players in a team have each their top competence important for the team to be able to solve the tasks they are working with.

A team also is defined by it`s a group of people, working together toward a common goal, a goal important for all the members of the team. The common goal can only be achieved if all the team members contribute to the process with their unique skills and competencies. You can say that in a team, the "whole" is bigger than "the parts". Individually, the players have unique skills but added together the team can achieve something the individual players can`t.

Research shows, that when people can contribute with unique skills to the work of a group, the individuals contributing will have the possibility to be recognized by the other members of the group. This recognition will develop the contributing players' self-esteem.

The recognition you can get from other players, if you contribute with unique skills, can be given in the form of specific signs or utterances. For example, if the coach is asking a question to the group, the players refer to a specific player to answer the question, as the player referred to, has a top competence in the relevant topic of the question. Another sign of recognition is that other players are listening respectfully when a player is talking about something in her area of competence. Recognition also is seen when players ask a specific player for advice regarding issues in the player's area of competence. In general, all signs that show players' trust and count on specific players to take control in specific situations can be interpreted as signs of recognition. As mentioned, this recognition will create the possibility for the player to develop higher self-esteem.

People with high self-esteem feel control and mastery when participating in activities in a specific environment. A badminton player with high self-esteem thus will experience, that she can participate and contribute in a good way to the activities in the group, and at the same time experience that she is recognized for unique skills and contributions. People developing high self-esteem, at the same time will develop intrinsic motivation, both regarding, involving themselves in the activities of the team and regarding playing badminton in general. Research shows, that when people are intrinsically motivated, they involve themselves in activities because they are fun. This means that intrinsically motivated badminton players probably will stay in the sport for a long time. It also means that intrinsically motivated players can reach a higher level of play than other players who are not intrinsically motivated.

If you want to work with team-based exercises is it important that the demands of the exercises make it necessary that different competencies have to be put into play, for the team to be able to solve the tasks contained in the exercises. The exercises should therefore contain periods where the players discuss which players can solve which tasks, trying to identify the top competencies of the different players. When I do team exercises, I very often do these as small competitions, where a team compete against itself or other teams. The element of competition can help motivate the players when trying to solve the task of the team as efficient as possible. I don't think that competition in itself is a negative thing, if only the competition is not spoken of as the most important factor, and if eventual rewards are only symbolic. It's important that intrinsic motivation, learning and development are the main focus also when doing competitions.

When I talk about team-based work in this book, on one hand, I talk about identifying overall unique competencies for the individual player, as the team in connection with this is all the players in the training group. At the same time, the individual exercises will identify situational unique competencies, as the team in this situation are the players working together in the specific exercise. In this way, the players continuously can experience recognition and develop higher self-esteem.

In the following section, I will describe how overall unique competencies can be put into play. After this, I will present a number of specific team exercises, aiming at developing the self-esteem of the players, and at the same time practising specific badminton competencies.

3.5 Specific team-based exercises

3.5.1 Identifying unique competencies

Before I, in this section, present a number of specific team-based exercises, I will shortly introduce 2 general but still rather specific actions, that aim at identifying the individual players` unique competencies. Concerning these overall unique competencies, the team is understood as all the players in the training group.

A) Team-based training rests on the premise that the individual player in the team can contribute to the work of the team with unique skills and competencies. Research shows, that people learn from watching and trying to copy other people who have specific skills. We learn from watching role models do their things. Therefore, it is a good idea to let players with special skills demonstrate and teach these skills to the other players. If the topic of the practice is "moving to the net after a contra shot in doubles", it is, as mentioned, a good idea to let the player whose top competence is this, demonstrate a situation where the specific situation takes place. Working in this way we achieve 2 things. First, the players in the team learn about the specific tactical situation, and secondly, the player demonstrating the situation is recognized for her unique contribution. The recognition will, as mentioned before, mean that the player will develop higher self-esteem, and as a result develop a higher level of play.

B) If a club has an ambition that part of the practice shall be team-based, it is necessary to start with identifying the individual players` top competencies. This can be done by having an initial meeting with the players, where they discuss their own and other players' top competencies. This process combined with the coach's eventual knowledge of the players will probably create the possibility to identify the individual players' unique competencies and special skills. As mentioned above it is a good idea to let players demonstrate their unique skills and use them as role models. Apart from this, it is a good idea to give the individual players a "title". The titles tell everybody else, what the top competence of the player is. For example, we could have a "reflection minister", who is the player that reacts fast and efficient when situations change on the court. Another example could be that we have a "captain" of the team. The role of "captain" is not a role we traditionally use much in badminton, but working in teams could be relevant to doing so. Working with "titles" like this is a way of delegating responsibility to the individual players, which again will increase the possibility for the players to be recognized by the other players, and as a result, develop higher self-esteem.

 As mentioned, these 2 general actions can help reinforce the effect of the specific team-based exercises I will present in the next section.

The aim of the exercises is, that the players continuously discuss and find out which player can contribute with what, to solve the task of the team in the most efficient way.

Working in this way will secure the players' experience that they are recognized for overall top competence. Also, the specific exercises will identify other areas the players will be responsible for, and in this way, help develops self-esteem.

3.5.2 Specific team-based exercises.

Exercise 123:

This exercise is a 3 against 3 exercise I call "badminton volley".

We play a match with normal point scoring on a singles court. The players on each side of the net have to hit the shuttle 1 time each, which means that the shuttle has to be hit 3 times, and the third shot has to return the shuttle to the other side of the net.

The rally starts up with an overhand service like in tennis, from the doubles service line at the back of the court. The third shot that returns the shuttle to the opponents` half, has to be hit behind the doubles service line at the back of the court. It`s OK that the player returning the third shot jumps across the service line to return the shuttle, as long as she doesn`t stand on the floor when she hits the shuttle.

Before the exercise starts up, the players discuss who is going to hit shots number 1, 2 and 3, as the 3 shots demand different technical skills from the players.

We play short sets to 5 or 7 points, and between the sets, the players can discuss tactics and evaluate if they have chosen the right players for the 3 shots. It is allowed between the sets to change which player is hitting which shot.

As the 3 shots demand different technical skills, the aim of the exercise is, that the individual players experience, that they are chosen to do a specific shot because of their special competencies. This will, as mentioned before, create the opportunity for the players to experience that they are recognized, and as an effect of this, develop self-esteem.

The team in this exercise will be the 3 players on the same side of the net.

Exercise 124:

In this exercise, we play 3 against 3 on a singles court.

The teams have to hit the shuttle 3 times before returning it to the other side of the net. The players on the team have to hit the shuttle 1 time each, and the rallies start up with a long single service.

The players have to hit the shuttle in 3 different ways. One player can hit a normal shot. The second player has to hit the shuttle with the "wrong" or the non-dominant hand, and the third player has to hit the shuttle with a part of the body, that is not the arm or the hand. The third shot that returns the shuttle to the opponents` side, has to be either with the "wrong" hand or with the body.

Before the exercise starts, the players have to discuss which player is doing which shot, and also in which order the shots shall be played. The players have to use the shot they have selected for the entire set, but the order the shots are played can be changed between the rallies, if only the third shot is always with the "wrong" hand or with a part of the body.

Again, we play short sets to 5 or 7 points. Between the sets, the players discuss their tactical choices, and they can change which players are doing which shots if they find it appropriate.

The exercise is a team-based exercise, as the team is the 3 players on the same side of the net.

Exercise 125:

This exercise is a variation from the previous exercise.

Again, the players are together 3 and 3, and the shuttle shall be hit 3 times on each of the net before it`s returned to the other side on the third shot. The players have to hit the shuttle 1 time each.

There are 3 ways you can hit the shuttle now. One player has to kick to the shuttle with the dominant foot. The second player has to kick to the shuttle with the non-dominant foot, and the third player can do a normal shot with the racket.

Before the exercise, the players on the team have to discuss who is going to do what. There is a free choice regarding which order the players hit the shuttle. The individual player has to do the return agreed for the whole set.

We play short sets to 5 or 7 points, and between the sets, the players discuss tactics and they can change which players are using which shots.

Again, the team is the 3 players on the same side of the net.

Exercise 126:

The good old "round the court" exercise can be used as a team exercise.

In this exercise, we play "round the court" in a competition between teams on different courts. For example, the exercise is done with 6 players on each team. The players now have to have different ways of hitting the shuttle. For example, it could be

- Only underhand shots
- Only overhand shots
- Only backhand shots
- Only shots with the non-dominant hand
- Only shots with both hands on the grip.

Before the exercise starts, the teams have to discuss which players have which tasks, to optimize the teams` performance. After this, we play around the court, and the team is finished when the shuttle is dropped on the floor. The team that finishes the latest wins the competition.

We play 2 – 4 matches, and between the sets, the teams discuss tactics and are allowed to change the tasks of the players.

Exercise 127:

"Around the court" can also as shown earlier in this book, be played around several courts at the same time.

For example, we have 10 players in this exercise, playing around the court on 2 courts. 8 players are on the 2 courts standing on each their half court in front of each other. At the net posts on each court, we have a player waiting to move into the court. When a player has made a shot to the partner on the other side of the net, she moves half a court to the right. The player waiting at the post moves into the court while the player on this court moves to the right. We have 4 shuttles in the air at the same time, 1 on each half-court.

We now define 10 different ways of returning the shuttle, from the same idea as in the previous exercise. The ways to return the shuttle can vary and should be adjusted to the level of the players.

Before the exercise, the team discusses who is going to do what, and where on the courts the different players shall be placed.

The exercise can be done as a competition where the team competes against itself, to see how long time they can keep the exercise going without dropping a shuttle on the floor. The exercise can also be done as a competition where the team competes against other teams or against the coach, as described in an earlier exercise.

Again, the exercise should be done 2- 4 times, so the team can discuss tactics, and have a chance to change the tasks and positions of the players.

Exercise 128:

This exercise is a competition where a number of teams compete against each other. We have 4 players on each team, and the team has to solve 4 tasks to finish the exercise. The 4 tasks are:

1) Hit the head of a racket placed in the "cross" at the service line at the net, with a short service.

2) Hit the head of a racket placed at the backline with a long high service.

3) Hit a racket head placed at the back line with a clear shot.

4) Hit a racket head placed on the middle of the court with a full smash.

The tasks have to be solved in order from 1 to 4.

As mentioned, the team compete against other teams, and the team has finished the exercise when all 4 tasks are solved.

Before the exercise starts, the team discusses who is going to solve which tasks, to optimize the possibility to win the competition.

The exercise should be done 2 – 4 times, so the teams can discuss technical and tactical issues, and maybe change the tasks of the players.

The exercise can vary in many ways depending on what technical tasks should be solved. In this way, the exercise can be adjusted to the player's age and level.

Exercise 129:

In this exercise, 2 teams are playing against each other.

We have, for example, 5 players on each team and each player has a task to solve. The 5 tasks could be:

- 1 player shall play without using long service.
- 1 player shall play without using backhand shots.
- 1 player shall play without using forehand shots.
- 1 player shall play without using net lob.

We play on a singles full or half court, depending on the number of players and courts, and also depending on the level of the players, as the exercise probably will be easier on a singles half court.

Before the exercise starts, the teams define an order of strength from 1 to 5. Number 1 on one team play against number 1 on the other team and so on. The teams also discuss which players will have which tasks, considering how to optimize the chance for the team to win the competition.

We play on time, for example, 10 minutes, and the team with the highest number of points wins the match.

It`s a good idea to do the exercise 2 – 3 times, so the teams can discuss tactics, and maybe change the tasks of the players if they find this appropriate.

The exercise can vary in a lot of ways, depending on the tasks the teams can choose between.

Exercise 130:

This exercise is a variation from exercise 129, as the tasks are a little more complex and challenging.

Again, we have 2 teams competing against each other, as we play singles on a singles full or half court.

We have, for example, 5 players on each team, and the teams have to put up an order of strength from 1 to 5. Number 1 from one team play against number 1 from the other team and so on.

Again, we have 5 tasks, 1 for each player. The tasks could for example be:

- Unprovoked errors mean minus 3 points for the player making the mistake.

- Clean winners – the shuttle hits the floor on the opponent's side, without the opponent touching it – means 3 points instead of 1.

- If the rally is won inside the first 6 shots, the player winning gets 3 points instead of 1.

- If the rally is won from a kill at the net, the player killing gets 3 points instead of 1.

- If the rally is won from a net spin shot that hit the top of the net, the player making the net shot gets 3 points instead of 1.

We play matches of 10 minutes, and the team with the most points win the match.

It's a good idea to do the exercise 2 – 3 times, so the teams can discuss tactics, and maybe change the tasks of the players if they find this appropriate

Again, the exercise can vary in a lot of ways, depending on the tasks the teams can choose between.

Exercise 131:

In this exercise, the players are together in teams of 4. Each team do the exercise on a singles court, competing against other teams.

The team has to hand out 4 shots, 1 to each player. For example, the shots could be a forehand shot, a backhand shot, an overhand shot and an underhand shot.

The team now has to see how many shuttles they can keep in the air at the same time. Before the exercise starts, the team discusses how they can solve the task, as the players can only use the shots handed out to them.

The exercise is done on time, for example, 3 minutes.

The exercise can be repeated 3 – 5 times, and the team discusses tactics between the repetitions and have the possibility to change which strokes the individual players have to use.

Again, the exercise can vary in many ways depending on the strokes the players can use.

Exercise 132:

In this exercise, 2 teams are competing against each other. For example, we have 5 players on each team, and the players play singles. The teams are put up in order of strength from 1 to 5, and number 1 on one team play against number 1 one on the other team and so on.

The game is "memory", as there, behind the courts of both teams are 13 playing cards, for example, the 13 harts, placed on the floor, and mixed with the neutral side upwards.

When a player has won a little match to 3 points, the player can run to the cards and turn one of them, so she can see the value of the card. The cards have to be turned in order from 1 to 13. If the first player who turns a card doesn`t turn the ace, the card is placed as it were with the neutral side upwards. When the ace is turned, it is placed as it were, but now with the picture side upwards and the team now have to find number 2.

However, before the players can turn a card they have to answer a question that is placed beside the cards. For the exercise, the coach has made questions in 5 categories, and before the exercise starts, the team has to decide which player has to answer which categories of questions.

The exercise is a team exercise, where players can contribute with unique skills by answering the questions. This means, that lower-level players can contribute important skills to the team, and thereby be recognized and develop higher self-esteem.

Exercise 133:

In this exercise, we play the old traditional game "tic-tac-toe".

We play a team match – 2 teams against each other, for example on 6 courts. The match consists of 6 singles matches, and we have different restrictions on the 6 courts. It could be restrictions like "box play", "singles half court", "only use underhand shots", "only use backhand shots", "play with the wrong hand" and "only play to the ditches on the court".

Before the game starts, the teams have to discuss which players will have which restrictions. The teams will not know how the other team delegates the tasks before the exercise starts.

When a player had won a little match to 3 points, she can run to 9 cones, set up in a tic-tac-toe pattern as shown below, and place a mark, for example, a shuttle at one of the 9 cones. Each team has 3 marks to place.

Figure 16.

134

The team that gets 3 cones in a row marked will win the match.

The exercise can vary in many ways depending on the restrictions of the courts. Also, the tic-tac-toe pattern can be expanded to, for example, 12 or 15 cones.

Again, it`s a good idea to do the exercise a number of times, so the teams between the matches can discuss which players should have which restrictions.

Exercise 134:

In this exercise, we play 3 against 3. The players on each team shall hold hands, thus the player in the middle holds hands with the other players. The players on each side of the middle have a racket in their free hand.

We play sets to 5 points on a singles court. Before the exercise starts and between the sets, the teams shall discuss which players will have which tasks, as the team can change the placement in the chain between the sets.

It will be appropriate if we on all the teams have players playing with the same hand, for example, right hand. If this can`t be done, it`s important that the teams playing against each other consist of two players playing with the right/the left hand and the third with the opposite hand. This is important to avoid one of the teams getting an advantage if both players with a racket can play with their dominant hand, and the other team can`t.

Exercise 135:

The exercise is a variation from exercise 134. Again, we play 3 against 3, and the players are holding hands.

We now define which shots the players with rackets can use. For example, one player has to make backhand shots, and the other player has to make underhand shots.

The exercise can vary in a lot of ways, depending on the shots selected for the exercise.

Exercise 136:

Again a variation from the previous exercises.

The players are holding hands, and we define the 2 shots the players with the rackets have to use.

In this exercise, the shuttle has to be hit 3 times on each side of the net, as the third shot returns the shuttle to the other side of the net.

The teams can decide for themselves in which order they hit the shuttle, as long as each player hits the shuttle 1 time. This means that the player in the middle shall hit the shuttle with a part of the body while holding hands with the other players.

Again, we play short sets, so the teams can discuss tactics and delegation of tasks between the sets.

CHAPTER 4

EXERCISES DEALING WITH HOW TO HANDLE MENTAL PRESSURE

4.1 A little about becoming nervous and practising how to deal with mental pressure on the court.

Most badminton players probably have experienced becoming nervous and feeling mental pressure in tournaments and training, and therefore are unable to play the game as they want to, and maybe are used to doing it. Often, players feeling mental pressure will force the game to get points fast with the risk of making easy mistakes. The opposite also happens meaning that the players feel paralyzed and play with no plan in the rallies. In general, the experience of pressure can mean, that players are not able to make appropriate choices in the rallies, which of course is the main condition for being able to do well on the court.

When you, as a badminton coach consider how you can practice the players' ability to handle mental pressure, you will often refer to sports psychologists who traditionally deal with problems like these.

In the sports psychological philosophy of Team Denmark, it says, that you can work with mindfulness and commitment training (ACT) to handle situations with stress and pressure. Focus on values like identity and meaning also will enable the athlete to cope with pressure properly. I agree that sports psychologists and the mentioned technics are efficient and relevant, especially at the elite level.

However, this approach indicates that there, in the daily badminton training, is no structured focus on practising and developing the players' ability to handle mental pressure in training and competition.

I will argue, that the ability to handle pressure can be practised equally with technical, tactical, and physical elements. This means, that we can practice our ability to handle pressure by making exercises that simulate situations where we feel the pressure. This means that the players get used to dealing with and reflecting upon these specific situations, and as a result of the reflection process, develop effective solutions for the next time you are in a situation where you feel pressure. This way of thinking, of course, is analogue to what I have written in this book regarding constructivism and reflection.

As described earlier, learning is an adaptive process, meaning a process where you through reflection and testing new possibilities for acting, improve your possibility of "surviving", or in other words handle future situations on the court in a way the situation demands.

In connection to this Team Denmark writes in their sports psychological philosophy, that increased awareness regarding your reactions, helps the athlete to handle discomfort, and keep the focus on what matters in competition. One way to create increased awareness regarding how to handle these situations is to create situations in training that simulate pressure in competition, and together with the coach and other players evaluate and discuss future possibilities for action. Kristoffer Henriksen, who is a professor in psychology at the University of Southern Denmark, says in connection with this that *"if you can predict the disturbances you will meet in competition, you can practice with that kind of disturbance, and get used to it"*. The disturbance will in this perspective, be the specific pressure in competition, which you try to recreate in practice.

In badminton matches during tournaments and team matches, you can argue the amount of mental pressure will increase depending on the specific situation. We can assume that the more matches you play in a tournament, the closer the players will be to the final victory, which probably will increase the experience of pressure for the individual player. The importance of team matches probably varies in the same way, for example, if the team plays for promotion or relegation, which again can increase the experience of pressure for the individual player. Likewise, the experience of pressure probably will increase during a match the closer you get to the end, especially if you play against an equal opponent. In the same way, specific rallies in a match can make the player feel pressure, for example, if the opponent shows signs of fatigue, which makes it important for the player not to make unforced errors.

It is important to bear in mind, that competition is a crucial element in these types of exercises, to simulate situations where pressure can occur. However, the competition itself can't overshadow the goal of the exercises, which is that the players properly handle mental pressure. Therefore, who wins or loses the competition in the exercises is not important when you evaluate the practice with the players.

As is the case for all exercises in this book, it's important to stress, that evaluation after the exercises is important. Both the coach and other players can take part in the evaluation after the exercises are finished. The evaluations of course aim at the players to reflect upon what happened in the exercise, and what can be changed in the future.

With a starting point in the above, I will, in the next section present a number of exercises practising the ability to handle mental pressure in matches. In my experience, the players find these exercises both fun and challenging, and it's only your imagination that set the limit for how you can develop exercises like this.

4.2 Specific exercises practising the ability to handle mental pressure on the court.

Exercise 137:

In this exercise, we play a team match, 2 teams against each other. We play a number of singles and doubles relevant according to the number of players and courts available.

We play 10 minutes matches and the total number of points the team wins on all courts counts. The team with the most points wins the match.

The individual player on the team probably will experience more mental pressure compared to playing a match by himself, as the team's chance of success now depends on the individual players` ability to win points. In this way, every rally will be important, no matter if the player wins or loses his match.

We play 2 or 3 team matches, and between the matches, the teams discuss tactics and are also allowed to change who is playing what.

Exercise 138:

Traditionally many badminton clubs have had a challenge board, where players could challenge each other, and play matches to get as high on the board as possible. The idea of a challenge board has always been controversial, as the concept can lead to unhealthy competition between players who are teammates, and who are expected to help each other.

However, regarding practising the ability to handle mental pressure, the concept of a challenge board can be relevant. The fundamental idea behind a challenge board is, that players can challenge other players that are higher ranked than themselves, for example, they can challenge players ranked up to 3 positions higher. It seems fair to assume, that the players will experience more pressure playing these matches, compared to normal practice.

If you do challenge matches like this, it's important always to keep the purpose of the matches in focus. Of course, it's important to win the matches, but the most important thing is to practice the ability to handle mental pressure. To secure this, we have to evaluate the matches focusing on how the players felt and dealt with the mental pressure.

Exercise 139:

A little simple exercise, regarding practising the ability to handle mental pressure, is that the coach appoints a match round in the training to be Olympic Finals, so the winners of the matches can call themselves Olympic Champions until the next time they do a match round like this.

The simple fact that you talk about something as being especially important probably will affect the amount of mental pressure felt by the players.

Exercise 140:

In this exercise, we play singles for 10 minutes periods.

The restriction in the exercise is that the player has to win 3 rallies in a row, to win a point. The players will, in this exercise experience, that the mental pressure will increase the closer they get to winning 3 points in a row. Probably the third rally in a series of won rallies will be experienced as more stressful than rallies 1 and 2.

We play 2 or 3 matches, and the players evaluate between the matches primarily on how to play under pressure.

Exercise 141:

This exercise is the same as exercise 140, apart from, we are now playing doubles. Again, the pairs have to win 3 rallies in a row to win a point.

The mental pressure in this exercise probably will be higher, as the individual players` eventual mistakes now also affect the partner.

Again, we evaluate between matches, focusing on how the players reacted to the pressure.

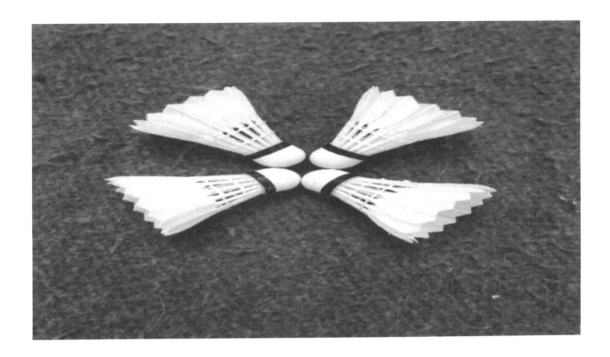

Exercise 142:

In this exercise, we play singles in short sets to 9 points.

The restriction in the exercise is that if a player wins 3 rallies in a row, the set is finished, and the player winning 3 rallies in a row wins the set.

We play, for example, for 30 minutes, and between each set, the players and the coach reflect upon tactics with a special focus on how to handle pressure. The player with the most won sets after 30 minutes is the winner of the exercise.

The experience of mental pressure in this exercise probably will be very high, as the players never can be sure to win the set, no matter what the score is.

Exercise 143:

Again, in this exercise, we play singles in 10 minutes periods.

The restriction in the exercise is that when the players make an unprovoked mistake, they get 3 minus points, and the opponent still gets 1 point. After the 10-minute play, the players can end up with a negative score.

As the players are punished hard when making unforced mistakes, the players probably will experience a lot of mental pressure doing the exercise.

Again, we play 2 to 3 matches so the players can reflect and evaluate between the matches.

Exercise 144:

This exercise is a progression from the previous exercise.

Again, we play singles in 10 minutes periods, and when players make unforced mistakes, they get minus 3 points.

However, if the players make "clean" winners, meaning hitting the shuttle to the opponents' floor without the opponent touching it, the player making the "clean" winner gets 3 points instead of 1.

You can argue that the amount of mental pressure in this exercise, compared to the previous exercise, will be higher, as the players are encouraged to take chances to win 3 points, risking minus 3 points for an unforced mistake.

As in all exercises in this book, it is important to evaluate in and after the exercise, so the players can reflect on how they acted and what can be changed in the future.

Exercise 145:

This exercise is the same as exercise 143, apart from now playing doubles instead of singles.

We can assume that the players feel more mental pressure in this exercise compared to exercise 143, as mistakes from the individual players now will affect their partners negatively.

Thus the exercise can be seen as a progression from exercise 143, as well as it can be an option for doubles players who don`t want to play singles.

Exercise 146:

The exercise is the same as exercise 144, apart from now playing doubles instead of singles.

Again, the players get minus 3 points for making unforced mistakes, and 3 points when making "clean" winners.

The mental pressure in this exercise probably will be higher, compared to exercise 144, as the players are encouraged to take chances risking being punished for making unforced mistakes.

As always, there should be time for reflection and evaluation between the small matches.

Exercise 147:

In this exercise, we play 2 against 2 on a singles court, and the players hit the shuttle on a shift like in table tennis doubles.

We play 2 – 3 matches of 10 minutes each. Between the matches, the players have time to discuss tactics and prepare for the next match.

The restriction of the exercise is that if a player makes an unforced mistake, the pair get minus 3 points, while the opponents get 1 point.

The experience of mental pressure in the exercise will probably be very high, as a player's mistakes have negative consequences for the partner as well.

Exercise 148:

In the exercise, the players are together 2 and 2. The players in the pair play singles against the other pair. The restriction is that the players in the pairing play the rallies on a shift, meaning the players play every second rally.

The pairing gets minus 3 points when making an unforced mistake, and again we play matches of 10 minutes.

The experience of mental pressure probably will be very high, as a player's mistakes will have negative consequences for the partner.

Exercise 149:

In this exercise, we play a team match, 2 teams against each other. We play a number of singles and doubles depending on the number of players and courts available.

We play 2 – 3 matches of 10 minutes, and between the marches, the players discuss tactics and prepare for the next match.

If players make unforced mistakes they get minus 3 points, and the opponents get 1 point.

The team with the most points after 10 minutes wins the match.

The mental pressure in this exercise probably is extremely high, as players' mistakes will have negative consequences for the whole team.

Exercise 150:

This exercise is a progression from exercise 149. Apart from getting 3 minus points when making unforced mistakes, the players now also get 3 bonus points when making a "clean" winner.

You can argue that the experience of mental pressure in this exercise will be even higher, compared to exercise 149, as the players now are encouraged to take chances and go for "clean" winners, with the risk of making unforced mistakes.

In these team exercises, it's a good idea that the evaluation between and after the matches is done between the players with input from the coach.

Exercise 151:

In the exercise, we play singles or doubles to 21 points without extension. However, the matches start with an 18 – 18 score, and we play without extension.

Even if these, in reality, are only set to 3 points, the italicization of the set being close to the end probably will increase the experience of mental pressure.

I have done this exercise myself, and in my experience, it has a large effect when it comes to creating pressure on the players.

Exercise 152:

In this exercise, we play singles or doubles depending on the number of players and courts available.

The exercise is done for 30 minutes, and we play sets to 11 points. The restriction here is, that when a player or a pair has made 3 unforced mistakes, the player making the 3 unforced mistakes loses, and the set is finished no matter what the score is. The player or the pair who has won the most sets after 30 minutes wins the match.

The experience of mental pressure probably will be very high, as you continuously risk losing the set, even if you are ahead on points.

The exercise can be adjusted to a different level of players just by changing the number of unforced mistakes it will take to lose the set.

Exercise 153:

This exercise is almost the same as exercise 152. The difference is that now the players can win the set by making 3 clean winners, and at the same time, lose the set by making 3 unforced mistakes.

As in previous exercises, we can assume that the experience of mental pressure in this exercise will be very high, as the players have to find the balance between attacking and playing safe.

Exercise 154:

In this exercise, we play a team match with 2 teams playing against each other, and we play singles and doubles appropriate to the number of players available. The exercise goes on for 30 minutes. In the 30 minutes, we play small 8 minutes team matches. If a player or a pair on the team makes 3 unforced mistakes during the 8-minute match, the match is finished, and the entire team loses the match.

If no players make 3 unforced mistakes during the 8 minutes, the team with the most points wins the match.

The team with the most match wins after 30 minutes win the competition.

The experience of mental pressure will be very high in the exercise, as mistakes from individual players will have negative consequences for the whole team.

Exercise 155:

This exercise is almost the same as exercise 154. The difference is, that if a player or a pair makes 3 clean winners in the 8 minutes, the team wins the match. The team still loses the match if a player or a team makes 3 unforced mistakes in the 8 minutes.

If none of the players makes either 8 winners or 8 mistakes, the team with the most points wins the match.

The team with the most matches won wins the competition.

Again, the experience of mental pressure will be very high, as the players have to find the balance between attacking and playing safe, and their choices will affect the whole team.

Exercise 156:

In this exercise, we play singles on a singles court. We play for 30 minutes, and in the 30 minutes, we play a number of short sets.

Besides the court, we place some playing cards with values between 1 and 5, the ace having the value of 1.

Before each set, the players pick a card, and the value is the number of points the player has to have to win the set. The opponent mustn`t know the value of your card. After each set, the players pick a new card.

In my experience, the exercise is very fun for the players, and the fact that they never know when a set is finished, increases the experience of mental pressure.

Exercise 157:

The exercise is the same as exercise 156, apart from we play doubles instead of singles.

The experience of mental pressure probably is higher in this exercise, as mistakes from the individual players will have negative consequences, not only for the player himself but also for his partner.

Exercise 158:

In this exercise, we use the playing cards again. We play singles in sets of 11 points. Before each set, the players pick a card from the pile beside the court. The cards have values from 1 to 13, and the value tells the players which number rally in the set is the joker for the player picking the card.

The joker means that if the players win the rally with the number on the picked card, they get 3 points instead of 1. For example, if a player picks a card valued at 8, she gets 3 points if she wins rally number 8 in the set.

In my experience, the players find the exercise fun, as it tickles the stomach, as you don`t know when the opponent can get 3 points.

The experience of mental pressure will be high because you don`t know the opponents' card, and especially they will feel the pressure when they have to play their joker rally.

Exercise 159:

The exercise is almost the same as exercise 158. The only difference is that we now play doubles instead of singles.

We can assume that the experience of mental pressure now is a little higher compared to exercise 158 because the players' mistakes in the joker rallies will have negative consequences also for the partner.

Exercise 160:

In this exercise, we play singles on a singles court in sets of 11 points.

Before each set, each player picks a card from the pile beside the court. The cards have values between 1 and 9, and the card, which is the joker, tells the players which number rally in the set they have to win, to get 3 points for clean winners subsequently.

The experience of mental pressure in this exercise is very high, as winning the joker rally means, that the players can get many points in the set.

Exercise 161:

This exercise is almost the same exercise as exercise 160. The difference is that we now play doubles instead of singles.

The mental pressure will probably be higher in this exercise compared to the previous, as mistakes from a player can have negative consequences also for the partner.

It's important, especially in doubles exercises, that the players discuss and evaluate between the sets to get the possibility to reflect and help each other regarding the next set.

Exercise 162:

In this exercise, we once again use the playing cards.

We play singles in matches of 10 minutes, and before each match, the players pick a card with values between 1 and 9. The card is the joker and tells the players which number rally they have to win to avoid getting 3 minus points for unforced mistakes afterwards.

The experience of mental pressure probably will be very high in this exercise, as a lost joker rally means, that the players will have difficulties winning the match. A lost joker rally in this way means, that the players will have to change tactics to avoid unforced mistakes.

Exercise 163:

This is almost the same exercise as exercise 162. The difference is that we now play doubles instead of singles.

As in previous exercises we can assume, that the mental pressure will be higher, as players' mistakes in the joker rally will have negative consequences also for the partner.

Exercise 164:

In this exercise, we once again use the playing cards, and now we increase the amount of mental pressure a little, compared to the previous exercises we used the cards.

We play for 30 minutes in total, and in this period, we play short sets to 8 points. Before each set, the players pick a card with values between 1 and 13, ace being 1 and king being 13. It`s important that the opponent doesn't know the value of the card. The card tells the players, which number rally is the joker. If the player wins the joker rally, the set is finished, and the player winning the joker rally is the winner of the set. The player winning the most set in 30 minutes is the winner of the exercise.

The amount of mental pressure is very high, as the players never know if the rally they are playing could be the last in the set.

Exercise 165:

Almost the same exercise as exercise 164. The difference is that we now play doubles instead of singles. As in the previous exercises, the experience of mental pressure will probably be higher, as mistakes and bad choices from the individual player will have negative consequences also for the partner.

Again, we must evaluate between sets, so the players can reflect on what has happened, and what they can do in the sets to come. It's appropriate that the coach is a part of the evaluation, so he can help facilitate the reflection, which can help develop the players` ability to create new ways of acting.

Exercise 166:

This exercise is a variation from the previous exercises. We play singles in sets to 8 points, and before each set, the players pick a card with values between 1 and 13. The card is the joker card, and the value of the card tells the players which number rally in the set is the joker rally. If the players lose the joker rally, they lose the entire set.

We can assume that the amount of mental pressure in this exercise is very high, as a lost joker rally means that even if you are ahead on points in the set, you lose anyway.

Exercise 167:

In this exercise, we play singles to 11 points. The restriction is that a rally won inside the first 6 shots means that the player winning the rally gets 3 points instead of 1. This means that each player has 3 shots to win the rally, to get the 3 points. The experience of mental pressure will probably be very high in this exercise, as the tempo in the rally will be very high at the beginning of the set, as we can assume that the players will try to play offensively, but at the same time risk making unforced mistakes, which will give the opponent 3 points.

Exercise 168:

This exercise is almost the same exercise as exercise 167. The difference is that we now play doubles instead of singles.

The mental pressure in this exercise will probably be higher, compared to exercise 167, as the service situation is a possibility to put pressure on the opponents from the start of the rally.

This specific exercise is not different from the normal doubles, which makes the tactical discussions between the players relevant for normal doubles matches at the same time we practice the ability to handle mental pressure.

We play 2 – 4 sets, and between the sets, the players evaluate and discuss tactics.

Exercise 169:

This exercise is inspired by tennis and the way we count the points in tennis. In the exercise, we play singles, and the players have to win 5 games to win the match.

In the first game, both players have to win 5 rallies to win the game. The loser of the first game only has to win 4 rallies in the next game, while the winner still has to win 5 rallies. This means that when a player loses a game, she has to win a rally fewer in the next game.

The match is finished when a player loses a game where she should have won only 1 rally.

It`s my experience that the players find this exercise fun, and the experience of mental pressure will increase the fewer rallies the players have to win to win the game.

Exercise 170:

This exercise is a variation from the "memory" exercise described in exercise 110 earlier in this book. Exercise 110 aimed to develop communicative skills. In this exercise, however, the goal is to practice handling mental pressure.

We a team match, 2 teams against each other, as we play a number of singles and doubles depending on the number of players and courts available. The teams rank in order of strength, both regarding singles and doubles. Number one of the one team always plays against number one from the other team. One team must always play the matches standing on one side of the net, and the other team stands on the other side of the net,

Behind each team's courts, the team places 13 playing cards inside an area of a maximum of 1 square meter, with the neutral side turned upwards. The cards are mixed so the team doesn't know which cards are where, and the pattern that the cards are placed in from the beginning has to be kept during the exercise. This means, that it is not allowed to turn or move cards to signal that the cards have already been turned. The task of the teams is to turn the cards in order from 1 to 13. If a player turns the first card, and it's not number one, the card is turned back with the neutral side upwards. When the ace – or number one – is turned, it stays with the value side upwards, and the team now has to find number 2. The team who turns all 13 cards first, is the winner of the exercise.

We now play short matches to 3 points on all courts. When a player or a pair wins a match, they can run to the cards and turn 1 card. If the same card, for example, number 7 is turned 3 times without being the right card, the match is finished, and the other team wins the match

The exercise demands that we have an observer at both piles of cards to control how many times the cards are turned.

The amount of mental pressure is very high in this exercise, as the individual players' mistakes can cost the whole team the victory in the match.

In exercises like this, it`s very important to keep the focus on the goal of the exercise, so winning or losing doesn`t become the most important thing. This is to avoid players becoming sad or angry if they make mistakes.

Again, it`s a good idea to do the exercise 2 – 4 times so the teams can discuss and evaluate between the matches.

Final Words

Writing a book is a difficult journey that takes a lot of help, time, and effort. I am incredibly appreciative of all the people who helped this endeavor succeed as I consider how it has come to an end.

I want to start by sincerely thanking my family for their unwavering support and love during this journey. Their assistance has been the cornerstone of my writing, and this project would not have been feasible without it.

The numerous friends and coworkers who have helped me along the road are also to be thanked. My thoughts and writing have benefited greatly from their support, criticism, and insights.

Aside from that, I want to recognize the significance of my personal experiences and knowledge, which have shaped and improved the concepts portrayed in this work. I am eternally thankful for how each struggle, each victory, and each lesson have enriched my writing and added to its richness and authenticity.

Those who have given me study materials, data, and information have been generous and knowledgeable, and I am appreciative of that. Their assistance has been crucial in helping me develop my thoughts and write with accuracy and precision.

In addition, I want to thank the academic and professional networks that have helped me throughout my journey. I've developed as a writer and expanded my thinking thanks to their mentorship, advice, and tools.

Finally, I want to thank the readers of this book, whose interest and comments have been the best rewards for my efforts. I write with passion and dedication because of your interest and encouragement, and I hope this book will have a significant impact on you.

In conclusion, the process of producing a book is one that involves the assistance and support of numerous people. I am appreciative of the support I have received from my friends, family, life experiences, personal knowledge, research, study, coworkers, and readers throughout this journey. I appreciate you joining me on this voyage, and I hope this work will inspire, enlighten, and make you happy.

Montyf O Chana